# The Short-Term
# Missions Boom

# The Short-Term Missions Boom

## A Guide to International and Domestic Involvement

## Michael J. Anthony, Editor

**Baker Books**

A Division of Baker Book House Co
Grand Rapids, Michigan 49516

Published by Baker Books
a division of Baker Book House Company
P.O. Box 6287, Grand Rapids, MI 49516-6287

Printed in the United States of America

### Library of Congress Cataloging-in-Publication Data

The short-term missions boom: a guide to international and domestic involvement / Michael J. Anthony, editor.
    p.  cm.
    Includes bibliographical references.
    ISBN 0-8010-0233-8
    1. Short-term missions. I Anthony, Michael J.
BV2061.S48   1994
266—dc20                                  94-26120

This book is dedicated to my wife, best friend, and ministry partner, Michelle. We fell in love while participating together on a short-term missions project to bring famine relief to Haiti in 1987. Since that time we have served together on short-term projects in the Dominican Republic, Mexico, Belize, and Kenya. The Lord has blessed me with a wife who enjoys the challenge of Third-World travel and ministering in unpredictable places. She has filled our home with laughter, creative memories, and two wonderful children: Chantel and Brendon. God truly gives the perfect gift to those who are willing to wait for the best.

# Contents

**Part 3   *Mission Projects Close to Home***

# Introduction

I write this introduction shortly after returning from the Dominican Republic. I brought a group of twenty-five people to participate in a short-term missions experience over spring break. I have led more than fifty short-term trips to developing countries over the years but none has compared with the blessings of this trip. They seem to get better and better.

In a real sense, this latest trip confirms why I felt the need to compile this book. I have experienced the life-changing effect that a short-term missions trip can have on a person. I have seen God touch the lives of my students through these experiences as well. Many will never be the same as a result of what they have seen and experienced. You cannot hold a dying child in your arms, look into its eyes, and not be shaken by the experience.

The purpose of this book is to help church leaders understand the process of conducting short-term mission trips. I believe the North American church has been derelict in its responsibility of bringing volunteers to the mission field. We send people to sponsoring organizations, raise money to help pay their way, and then try to remember to pray for them while they are gone. The big problem occurs when they return.

Many times these people are overwhelmed by what they have seen and experienced but are lost when it comes time to channel that experience back into their local church. We may give them a token five-minute spot in an evening service to share their experience with us. But when it comes to really influencing the life of the church, their short-term trip is usually buried under a host of other activities and events. Eventually they feel out of place and they get the impression that missions is all right for a few people, but it isn't important in the life of the church as a whole.

The best way to conduct short-term missions in the local church is for one of the pastors to take the volunteers to the mission field himself or herself. With this approach, the entire church is swept into the missions experience; when the group returns, the influence is far greater on the church as a whole. The difficulty in this ideal scenario is that most local church pastors are not aware of how to facilitate such a mission venture. This book is written to remedy that lack of awareness.

There is nothing mystical about leading a short-term missions trip. As is true of most ministry experiences, you want to be sure that you are well prepared for the unexpected. But the key to a successful trip is quality preparation and planning. Each chapter in this book is designed to answer practical questions and to provide real-life answers. Each is written by a practitioner who knows his or her subject well. Let me introduce you to some of my friends who have contributed to this book.

Part 1 is designed to help the church leader instill a vision and awareness of world needs. Nobody can do this better than the author of chapter 1, Tony Campolo. He was recently at Biola University and rocked our campus in a way that is characteristic of Tony. He is one of our school's favorite speakers because he isn't afraid to "tell it like it is" even if it gets some people upset. May his tribe increase!

Chapter 2 is written by Jim Burns, a friend who is no stranger to the field of youth ministry and short-term missions. Jim leads a national organization committed to giving youth leaders across America the tools they need to effectively minister for Christ. He is a dynamic communicator and a gifted writer. His chapter on "Igniting Volunteers to Become World Christians" is thought-provoking and straightforward. Jim's heart is missions and bringing young people to the mission field.

Paul Borthwick, a prolific author and missions specialist, writes his chapter on the topic of "Developing a Christian World View in Your Church." Paul can speak from experience since he also serves as the missions pastor at his church, Grace Chapel, in Lexington, Massachusetts. Paul is a rare church leader who can say with boldness, "If you want to know how a world Christian lives, follow me."

He speaks from experience about how to motivate and challenge members of the local body of Christ.

I wrote chapter 4, "Focusing on Priorities: People versus Projects," to deal with some of the tough issues associated with short-term mission assignments. I answer questions such as, *Is this project worth the money it will take? Is this project worth the amount of investment that it will require from my group? How do I know that this project is really needed? Is it wrong for me to expect to get something from this experience myself?* I share some painful lessons that I have learned from doing short-term missions projects over the years.

Judy TenElshof writes from her experience as a professional marriage and family counselor and a professor at Biola University. She has participated in short-term missions trips and knows the kinds of stress and pressures they can produce. Her insights into the recruitment and selection process are valuable and needed by members of the church missions committee. I applied the contents of her chapter for the recruitment and screening of my latest short-term team. These methods work and I recommend them to you without hesitation.

Part 2 of this book deals with the issues that are related to preparing your church team for international missions involvement. Such a venture is not for the faint of heart, but with these practical suggestions one can enter the experience with more understanding and clarity of purpose.

The first chapter in this section is on fund-raising. It is written by two nationally known short-term missions writers. Their popular book *Vacations with a Purpose* has become one of the most beneficial books on short-term missions that has been published in this decade. Kim Hurst and Chris Eaton speak from experience and will give you practical guidelines and suggestions for fund-raising ideas that really work.

Ken Garland has written a number of excellent articles for *Youthworker* journal. With more than twenty years of church ministry experience, Ken knows how to work through a church board to accomplish effective ministry. Ken will help the short-term missions group leader see things from the perspective of the church board and senior pastor. After all, their approval is critical to the overall success of your trip.

Dennis Kasper writes chapter 8 based on his experience as an attorney specializing in church liability issues and also as a deacon at First Presbyterian Church of Hollywood, California. Dennis knows the liability issues of church ministry first-hand, for he was at the church when it experienced a tragic bus accident some years ago. This essential chapter needs serious consideration. The threat of litigation has seriously curtailed some church-sponsored foreign missions trips, and this chapter is designed to help the church leader prepare for any problems that may arise. When I was an associate pastor of a church about ten years ago I hired Dennis to design a liability release form that my church could use with confidence for our young people going to Mexico on weekend missions trips. An updated version of this form is included in his chapter and is well worth the cost of this book!

Jack Larson is well known across North America as the founder and executive director of World Servants, a missions organization specializing in short-term missions trips around the world. Although Jack now serves as a consultant who designs short-term mission trips, few people write with Jack's extensive experience in the field of short-term missions. Jack has built hospitals, medical clinics, orphanages, churches, and community centers all over the world. He knows short-term missions and has networked with dozens of short-term mission agencies in his capacity as a missions consultant.

I first met Samuel Melo, the executive director of Youth for Christ in the Dominican Republic, when I led a short-term experience in that country in 1986. Samuel has coordinated short-term trips for churches and organizations coming from all over North America. His unique perspective as a field director will provide you with a host of practical guidelines as you prepare your own trip.

The last chapter in this section is written by one of my best friends, Carolyn Koons. She is the executive director of the Institute for Outreach Ministries (IOM) at Azusa Pacific University. Every year over Easter vacation Carolyn brings students to Mexicali, Mexico, for a week of ministry to poor communities. This past Easter vacation, her organization brought more than five thousand students to Mexico. Nobody knows training and trip preparation like Carolyn, which is why I asked her to write this chapter. IOM has built hospitals, jungle airports, clinics, and churches in a host of countries around the world.

Part 3 shifts the focus from international missions involvement to local missions. As the director of Mariners Local Outreach at her church, Karen Taulien knows home missions. While I served on staff at Mariners Church I had the opportunity to watch Karen in action. Most churches give only token involvement to home missions. Mariners Church in Newport Beach, under Karen's leadership, puts on a home missions program that is second to none in the nation. Karen explains how to start a home missions program in your local church and walks you through all of the various issues related to this important subject.

Noel Becchetti is the director of ministries for the Center for Student Missions. Noel has been involved in urban ministries for many years and speaks from experience. The inner city is no place for the novice. His job is taking suburban students into the inner city for a plunge into reality. If you are a pastor of a local church and want a glimpse at inner-city life, then a short-term experience with Noel is a must. His chapter on visiting the inner city makes for exciting reading.

Bill Wilson and Chris Blake share a common vision of reaching urban children for Christ. Bill is the senior pastor and Chris is the Sunday school director at Metro Church in Brooklyn, New York. Bill has been involved in inner-city missions for more than twenty years. His church's Sunday school program goes out into the streets of the inner city and ministers to more than fourteen thousand individuals every week! Bill and Chris share their vision for how your church can join in their venture of reaching the inner city with the message of hope and redemption. Don't let the size of their ministry scare you. It started out with just one car and a couple of people whose hearts were sold out for God. Your church can have the same kind of ministry if your heart is open to it.

The chapter entitled "Come Play for a Day" is designed around a program that one of my students, Pam Reed Allison, developed at Biola. It is a creative and simple approach to local missions. It doesn't take a theological degree to reach the needs of people in urban areas. Most of the time it just requires a heart filled with compassion. Many Biola students have been involved in this program and Pam lays out the details clearly enough for your church to replicate it in your own setting.

The last chapter is written by Todd Alexander, one of my former college roommates, who founded an organization to train local churches in the area of world hunger awareness. World hunger sounds like such an overwhelming concept. Todd's material is very "user friendly." Any pastor could incorporate his materials into a church and find that they work. The result will be a sensitivity toward those in physical need and an appreciation for all that God has given to us in North America.

The annotated bibliography was developed by John Sung, my research assistant this year at Talbot Seminary. I appreciated his willingness to compile this wealth of material and to give such careful attention to the details of bibliographic research. You will find a wealth of materials for further reading in this section.

I would also like to express my appreciation to my secretary, Linda Paek, for her assistance in preparing the material in the directories at the end of the book.

This book flows out of a passion that we have for taking volunteers to the mission field on short-term experiences. As college professors and church pastors we have had the opportunity of seeing God change people's lives through short-term mission involvement. It is our prayer that you will gain confidence in your ability to lead short-term missions trips as you digest the material in this book.

If you have further questions about how to lead short-term mission trips, contact any of the authors listed in this book at the church or organization where they work. That is why I have provided the reader with specific information about each author's location. Call me at Biola University/Talbot Seminary if there is anything I can offer to help make your church missions experience successful.

Michael J. Anthony, Ed.D., Ph.D.
October 1994

# Part I

# Developing the Vision

As a church leader you probably already know why you want to get others involved in short-term missions. Perhaps you participated on a short-term trip while you were in high school or college and you have experienced the life-changing effects that such a trip can produce. Now you want others to share that experience as well.

The challenge of communicating your vision for short-term mission involvement is what part 1 is all about. Each chapter is designed to help you lay the groundwork for mobilizing your church for short-term mission involvement. These chapters will help you formulate your vision, communicate it to your church members, broaden your world view of Christianity, decide on what type of mission trip to invest in, and then help you begin to plan for mission action.

# Challenging the Church with Missions

*Tony Campolo*

Two thousand years ago they nailed Jesus to the cross. Two thousand years ago, they spiked him to the Roman gibbet. Two thousand years ago, as he died, something miraculous happened. Like a sponge, he absorbed the sins of every one of us. Like a sponge, he took the sins of the world onto himself and made them his own. Two thousand years ago, Jesus died on the cross. He who knew no sin became sin. The good news is that all who believe in him and trust in him will not be punished for their sin because on the cross he was punished in our place.

This chapter is adapted from *Urban Mission: God's Concern for the City*, edited by John E. Kyle. ©1988 by Intervarsity Christian Fellowship of the USA. Used by permission.

Not only that, God forgot our sins. Our sins were blotted out, says the Scripture, buried in the deepest sea, remembered no more. I don't know about you, but I would hate to go to heaven if God remembered.

Can't you just see me, standing before the judgment seat and the Lord saying, "Tony, we've been waiting for you." I don't know if they have a Tony book, but if they open it up, I've got good news: There won't be any of the rotten, dirty things that I've done written in the Tony book. It is forgotten.

There's one thing more. Besides taking our sin on himself and forgetting we ever sinned in the first place, he also "imputeth unto us his righteousness." That's out of the King James Version. I am an old King James man, and unfortunately many new versions don't have good words like "imputeth". It's a great word. It means he gives us the credit for all the good things that he ever did.

I can't wait to get to glory. When they open my book, they're going to have under the name Tony Campolo all the good stuff that Jesus ever did. I'm going to be credited for it. It's going to be imputed unto me.

I wish my wife no harm, but I want her there when I arrive because I know when they start reading all the good stuff that Jesus ever did, she's going to say, "You didn't do all of that." I'm going to say, "It's his book." I can say joyfully, "There is therefore now no condemnation for those who are in Christ Jesus" (Rom. 8:1 RSV).

Perhaps you're thinking, "That's an interesting theological perspective. But there are varying views on salvation. There are Buddhist views and Confucian views and Marxist views. How can you be so narrow-minded to say that your view, the biblical view, the Christian view, is the only view?"

I was on an airplane coming from California to Philadelphia. I sat down next to this guy. It was the red-eye special, one o'clock in the morning, and he wanted to talk. He said, "What's your name?" I said, "Tony Campolo." He said, "What do you do?" When I don't want to talk I say, "I'm a sociologist." And they say, "Oh, that's interesting." But if I really want to shut them up, I say, "Oh, I'm a Baptist evangelist." Generally that wipes the guy out right on the spot. So, not wanting to talk at all, I said, "I'm a Baptist evangelist."

He said, "Do you know what I believe? (I could hardly wait.) I believe that going to heaven is like going to Philadelphia. There are many ways to Philadelphia. Some go by airplane. Some go by train. Some go by bus. Some drive by automobile. It doesn't make any difference how we go there. We all end up in the same place."

I said, "Profound," and went to sleep.

As we were coming into Philadelphia, the place was fogged in. The wind was blowing, the rain was beating on the plane, the wings were shaking, and it looked like the whole plane was going to come apart.

Everyone was nervous and tight. As we were circling in the fog, I said to the theological expert on my right, "I'm certainly glad the pilot doesn't agree with your theology."

"What do you mean?"

I said, "The people in the control booth are giving instructions to the pilot, 'Coming north by northwest, three degrees, you're on beam, you're on beam, don't deviate from beam.' I'm glad the pilot's not saying, 'There are many ways into the airport. There are many approaches we can take. There are many ways we can land this plane.' I'm glad he is saying, 'There's only one way we can land this plane, and I'm going to stay with it.'"

There is no other name whereby we can be saved except the name of Jesus. This Jesus who died two thousand years ago on the cross, this Savior who is the only way to deliver us from sin, is a resurrected Jesus. And he comes to us even today. He is alive. He is here. And a lot of people here need to accept him, and a lot of people here need to surrender to him.

## The Cultural Jesus

But often people are turned off to Jesus because they don't really know what he's like. In the first chapter of Romans it says, "For since the creation of the world God's invisible qualities—his eternal power and divine nature—have been clearly seen, being understood from what has been made, so that men are without excuse. For although they knew God, they neither glorified him as God nor gave thanks to him, but their thinking became futile and their foolish hearts were darkened. Although they claimed to be wise, they became fools and exchanged the glory of the immortal God for images made to look like mortal man and birds and animals and reptiles. Therefore God gave them over in the sinful desires of their hearts to sexual impurity for the degrading of their bodies with one another. They exchanged the truth of God for a lie, and worshiped and served created things rather than the Creator" (Rom. 1:20–25).

That is not a description of some preliterate society. That is a description of American society. Ours is a society that has taken Jesus and has recreated him in our own image. When I hear Jesus being proclaimed from the television stations across our country, from pulpits hither and yon, he comes across not as the biblical Jesus, not as the Jesus described in this book, but he comes across as a white Anglo-Saxon Protestant Republican. A Jesus who incarnates what we are, rather than a Jesus that incarnates the God of eternity—this is not the Jesus who can save.

When I was teaching at the University of Pennsylvania, students would say, "I don't believe in God."

I would always say to them, "Describe to me this Jesus that you don't believe in. Describe to me this God you don't believe in." They usually thought that was a stupid question. But I would force them to answer it. And when they finished telling me what God was like, I would always congratulate them and say, "You're halfway to becoming a Christian because the greatest barrier to confronting and loving the real Jesus is being confused by the cultural description of Jesus that has emerged in our society."

We have in fact done something terrible. God created us in his image, but we have decided to return the favor, and we have created a God who is in our image.

You have a decision to make. Which God, which Jesus, do you choose to follow? Do you choose to follow the Jesus described in the Bible, the Jesus who died on the cross for your sins, the Jesus who was resurrected? Or do you choose to look at another Jesus, a Jesus that is created by the culture and that embodies and reflects our values?

## What Car Would Jesus Buy?

What is the difference between the two? The differences are pronounced. The Jesus of the Bible differs from the Jesus of culture in what he asks of you. The biblical Jesus bids you come and give everything that you are, everything that you have to him. The biblical Jesus says, quite simply, "Read my book. Read my Scripture. Come learn of me. And then in your everyday life, be like me." Let this mind be in you which is also in Christ Jesus. To be a follower of the biblical

Jesus is to do exactly what the biblical Jesus would do if the biblical Jesus were in your shoes and in your circumstances.

Nothing is more controversial than to be a follower and a disciple of Jesus Christ. Nothing is more dangerous than to live out the will of Jesus in today's contemporary world. First, it will change your whole monetary lifestyle. What you do with your money will change.

People ask me, "What do you mean? Are you suggesting that if I follow Jesus I won't be able to go out and buy a BMW?" You got it! I know a lot of people who own BMWs. When they really get godly, they will repent of their BMWs because BMWs are luxury cars that symbolize conspicuous consumption instead of compassionate concern for the sufferings of the world.

Supposing that Jesus had to buy a car since there aren't donkeys on the highways anymore. If he had forty thousand dollars and knew about the kids who are suffering and dying in Haiti, what kind of car would he buy? This is not irrelevant. This is where Christianity needs to be applied.

You've got to buy what Jesus would buy. You've got to dress with the kind of clothes that Jesus would dress in. There's no room for conspicuous consumption. This culture has in fact conditioned you to want more and more stuff you don't need so that while you are consumers of God's wealth, the hungry of the world suffer and the hungry of the world die.

It's time to repent of our affluence. Christians have lost the heart of the poor. Dr. Hestenes, my boss, once said, "You're not a Christian in the full sense of the word until your heart is broken by the things that break the heart of Jesus."

At the college where I teach I urge all of our sociology majors to go to the Dominican Republic or Haiti on study tours during the month of January. I want them there. The first time I took a group of students there we stayed in a filthy, dirty home in a slum. In the early morning the priest of the village invited us to walk with him. There was a flu epidemic. I had never seen anything like it. In the United States and Canada when people get the flu, they miss school. But when people are extremely malnourished and they get the flu, they die. As we wandered through the mud paths of the slum, mothers came out of their shacks that morning carrying the corpses of the children who had died during the night.

We went to the edge of the town, and we dug a ditch. And into the ditch we dropped these dead kids. We looked across the ditch as the priest prayed his prayer and the women screamed as only they can scream in the Dominican Republic.

I saw one of my students who was a basketball player. He was always macho. But he didn't look macho that day. Tears were streaming down his cheeks. His fists were clenched. His chin was trembling. And I knew, I knew that his heart had been broken by the things that broke the heart of Jesus. Blessed are they that mourn. Tony, are you suggesting that you can't be rich and be a Christian at the same time? I'm not the guy that dreamed up the line that it's harder for rich people to enter the kingdom of heaven than for a camel to go through the eye of a needle. That was somebody else. Tony, you're going to insult rich people. Do you have this world's goods? And can you see somebody with a desperate need and hold on to what you have while they suffer and die? If that's the case, 1 John 3:17–18 asks, "How then can you say you have the love of God in your heart?" That's what I'm asking.

If this offends you, be offended. Reject Jesus if you must, but you dare not take the biblical Jesus and turn him into something that he is not. He is the Jesus that confronts you and asks, "Are you willing to lay it on the line?" For unless a man, unless a woman, denies himself or herself, he or she cannot enter the kingdom of heaven.

I worry about a church that has forgotten what the Bible teaches. We evangelicals work overtime proving that the Bible is inerrant, and after we do, then we refuse to accept what it says. It not only says we have to have a new attitude toward wealth, it means we have to be radical in all kinds of ways.

## The Dangerous Jesus

When I became a Christian, the Korean War was in progress. It was an incredible experience because I didn't know whether or not to accept the draft. I had a conversation with a colonel, and we argued back and forth.

He said to me, "What's your problem?"

"My problem is I want to do what Jesus would do."

"Could you get in a plane, fly over an enemy village and drop bombs?"

I said, "I could get in the plane. I could fly over the enemy village. But when I was about to release the bombs, at that moment I would have to say, 'Jesus, if you were in my place, would you drop the bombs?'"

I remember the colonel yelling back to me, "That's the dumbest thing I've ever heard. Everybody knows Jesus wouldn't drop bombs!" That colonel probably knew more about Jesus than most Baptist preachers that I know.

Tony, this is getting upsetting. What you are talking about now is getting politically dangerous. But when did Christianity cease being politically dangerous? We are looking for a new breed of Christians who will come to the Sermon on the Mount and live it out with a radical commitment. The world urgently needs people radically committed to the biblical Jesus.

The cultural Jesus will create a church very different from the biblical Jesus. The church that is generated by the cultural deity that we have dreamed up out of our Protestant imagination is an honorary chairperson of a static institution. The biblical Jesus is the leader of a revolutionary movement that is destined to challenge this world and transform it into the kind of world that God willed for it to be.

If you get involved with this Jesus, you are going to become a dangerous person. If they send you to South Africa, you will not be able to tolerate the injustice of oppression that exists in that place. You will raise questions when our armies march off to war in places like Nicaragua. You will become a person who becomes dangerous because this church is committed to justice.

I am looking for a church that sends people into every avenue of life—into business, into the arts, into the educational sector, into the entertainment world—to be the revolutionary leaven that transforms the world. The task of the church is not to get ready for heaven. It's to communicate the kingdom of heaven in the midst of this world. The kingdom of this world will become the kingdom of our God.

When I read the life of John Wesley and hear about the great Wesleyan revivals (which incidentally were initiated by students), I realize that Christianity can be an instrument for nonviolent change in a world that needs to be changed. When I read the stories of Charles Finney, the great revivalist of the 1800s, I realize that Jesus can be an infusing presence that transforms the world today as he did back then. The anti-slavery movement, the abolitionist movement, the feminist movement were all born out of the revivals of Charles Finney.

This is a historic moment because God wants to raise up a generation of men and women who will enter into every sector of society as agents of change, transforming the world into the kind of world he wills for it to be.

Is it always nonviolent? Yes, I believe it is. I believe we must stand up for truth and speak the prophetic word of God.

That's what I loved about Martin Luther King Jr. He came marching out of Selma, and he meets that old Bull Connors. And there they are. Bull Connors has his guns. Bull Connors has his clubs. Bull Connors has his troops. And King and his followers got down on their knees and prayed. There is nothing more vulnerable than a person on his knees in prayer. And at the count of ten, Connors and his troops marched in, and they bashed in the heads of King's followers, and I saw them battered and beaten and plastered all over that road. I knew—as I saw that on live television—that God had just won, that the civil rights movement had just won.

I know you're thinking, "How do you figure it won? They got their heads bashed in. They got stomped. They got kicked. They got killed." You're right. But we Christians have a nasty habit of rising again.

## The Love of Power

I want a church that changes the world not from a position of power but from a position of love and commitment. I get scared about Christians today because they are on power trips. We think that if we get enough power, if we get enough people in office, if we take over America, we can force America to be righteous. Why didn't Jesus ever think of that? I believe that we have to change the world with the weapons of the church and not the weapons of the world. We have another style, another way. It's loving servanthood. It's giving ourselves, it's moving in, it's caring, it's loving, it's redeeming, not destroying.

I can understand power because everybody loves power. I love power. One day when I was coming home from the University of Pennsylvania where I used to teach, I came down the expressway, and just as I crossed Cityline Avenue, I heard this kerplunk, ker-plunk. A flat tire. So I pulled over and jacked up the car. As I was changing the tire, I was listening to the radio which started to broadcast from the traffic helicopter. "Well, ladies and gentlemen, they're not going to get home tonight. They're backed up on the expressway all the way to Montgomery Avenue. They're standing still both directions on Cityline. The city of Philadelphia is at a virtual standstill."

I wondered to myself, "What has brought the city of Philadelphia to a standstill? What has frozen the fair City of Brotherly Love? Why has Frank Rizzo's town suddenly been paralyzed?"

Then the announcer said, "There is a brown car just west of Cityline Avenue." That's me! That's my car! Little Tony Campolo has got the city of Philadelphia standing still! Mothers can't get home. Children are crying for their fathers. Business deals are falling through. Lovers are not meeting, and I am making it happen! Who of us is immune to the lure of power? Who cannot be seduced by it? But the biblical Jesus is not into power. The biblical Jesus gave up power. He could have forced the world to be righteous, could he not? Instead he comes and infuses people with his Spirit and calls on them to live sacrificially in this world.

## A Hidden People

If I've been a little controversial, let me get very controversial. I have a friend in Brooklyn who is a pastor. He has a church in a dying community. Whenever I want a good story, I always call him because he always has good stories, even though he doesn't know it. I steal all his material.

"What happened last Tuesday?" I asked.

"Oh, that was weird," he said. "I had a funeral."

You see, he's a guy who makes so little that he has to do funerals to make a few bucks to keep himself going. He said the local undertaker had called with a funeral and nobody wanted to take it because the guy had died of AIDS. So he took the funeral.

"What was that like?"

"When I got there, it was weird. There were about twenty-five or thirty homosexuals sitting there. They sat there frozen with their hands on their laps. Their eyes were riveted straight ahead. They looked neither to the right nor to the left. I read some Scripture. I said some prayers. When the funeral was over, we went out and got into automobiles and drove out to the cemetery.

"I stood there at the edge of the grave as the casket went into the hole. Once again I read some Scripture. Once again I said some prayers. And when I had said the benediction and turned to leave, I realized that none of these homosexual men had budged. I turned back and said, 'Is there anything else I can do?'

"And one of them said, 'Yes, there's something else you can do. I haven't been to church for years. Actually I was looking forward to the funeral because I always love to hear them read the Twenty-third Psalm. Pastor, would you read the Twenty-third Psalm?' So I read the Twenty-third Psalm.

"When I finished another man said, 'There's a passage in the Book of Romans, and it says that nothing can separate us from the love of God. Do you know that passage?' And I read to those homosexual men, 'Nothing can separate you from the love of God. Neither height nor depth, nor things present, nor things to come, nor principalities nor powers, nothing—nothing can separate you from the love of God—nothing can separate you from the love of God.' And I stood there near the grave reading to these homosexual men passages of Scripture upon request for almost an hour."

When I heard that, I cried. I really cried because I knew these men are hungry for the Word of God but will never set foot inside a church because they believe that the church despises them. And they're right.

Am I approving of the homosexual lifestyle? Certainly not! All I'm saying is, When are we going to start loving the people that nobody else will love?

Somebody asked me, "If you were the pastor of a big inner-city church, what would you do?" They asked me that at a press conference yesterday. I said quite simply, "I would ask the church to mortgage the building, take the money and build a hospice for AIDS victims because I think we need to say something to the homosexual community."

There are Spanish-speaking people, black people, Italian people in the inner city. I'm here to tell you there are approximately nine to ten million homosexuals, and the church of Jesus Christ has forced them to become a hidden people. It's about time that, without approving of sin, we love people.

I'm looking for a whole new mission enterprise. I'm looking for Christians who will set up Christian hospices for AIDS victims, for young men and women who will become doctors and nurses to take care of these people that some of our more secular doctors and nurses won't touch. It's time for Christians to create a daring church—a church that dares to love.

## To Boldly Go Where No Man Has Gone Before

Lastly, the cultural Jesus only asks us to be reverent and to be religious. I am not calling you to be religious. I am calling you to take your life and say today, "Jesus, I love you. I love you so much, I want you to take my life, and I want you to use it to do something splendid. I want you to send me to those places where you need me to go. I'm here. Take me. If it's Africa, it's Africa. If it's Philadelphia, it's Philadelphia. If it's Buenos Aires, it's Buenos Aires. If it's Calcutta, it's Calcutta. I'll go where you want me to go, dear Lord. I'm yours."

The biblical Jesus wants to employ you in the place where he can use you to the optimum level. Why is that overseas? Because America is overstaffed. We have so many people coming out of colleges and universities these days that society can't absorb them all. You don't have to go to work for General Motors. It'll survive without you. You don't even have to be a doctor in the United States; they've got enough. You certainly don't have to add to the supply of American lawyers.

What I love about *Star Trek* was the starship Enterprise skipping out into the darkness, and the voice saying, "Challenged to boldly go where no man has gone before." I'm here to call you to go where no one's ever gone, to do what no one's ever done, to be what no one's ever been. Being a missionary is hard. But most of the alternatives are dull. If you want to be a Yuppie, that's OK. It's just boring. What do they do? Work all week, come home, sit in the jacuzzi and tell each other it's wonderful.

In the last scene of *Death of a Salesman,* when they lower Willie Loman into the grave, his wife says, "Bif, Bif, why did he do it? Why did he kill himself? Why did he commit suicide? Why did he do it, Bif?"

And Bif says, "Ah shucks, Mom. Ah shucks, he had all the wrong dreams. He had all the wrong dreams." If there's anything that can be said about this generation, it's that you've got all the wrong dreams.

If you want to be a schoolteacher, why be in a place where they don't really need you? Why not let God take you and place you where you are absolutely essential? If you want to be a doctor, why not go where you're desperately needed? Why would anyone want to be a doctor where half of your patients aren't even sick when you can go to the place where the life and death of hundreds of people will be hanging on you daily?

I'm with old Oswald Smith. I don't see why anybody should hear the gospel twice before everyone has had a chance to hear it once. Give your lives over to Jesus. The needs are so horrendous. If you think you can't do it, you're crazy.

I was asked to be a counselor in a junior-high Christian camp. Everybody ought to be a counselor in a junior-high camp just once. If any Roman Catholics are here, you're right, there is a purgatory. We tried everything to get through to these kids what the gospel was all about. But nothing worked. Junior-high kids' concept of a good time is picking on people. And in this particular case, at this particular camp, there was a little boy who was suffering from cerebral palsy and they began to pick on him.

They picked on little Billy. Oh, they picked on him. As he walked with his uncoordinated body, they would line up and imitate his grotesque movements. I watched him one day as he asked in his slow drawn-out speech, "Which way is the craft shop?" And the boys, mimicking his speech and movements, answered, "It's over there, Billy." And they laughed at him. I was irate.

But my furor reached its highest pitch on Thursday morning when it was Billy's cabin's turn to give devotions. They had appointed Billy to be the speaker. They wanted to get him up in front to make fun of him. And as he dragged his way to the rostrum, you could hear the giggles rolling over the crowd. And it took little Billy almost five minutes to say, "Jesus . . . loves . . . me. . . . And . . . I . . . love . . . Jesus." When he finished, there was dead silence. I looked over my shoulder, and there were junior-high boys bawling all over the place. A revival broke out.

As I travel all over the world, I find missionaries and preachers everywhere I go who say, "Remember me, I was converted at that junior-high camp." We had tried everything. We even imported baseball players whose batting averages had gone up since they had started praying. But in the end God chose not to use the superstars. He chose a kid with cerebral palsy to break the spirits of the haughty. He's that kind of God.

Give your life to Jesus no matter what you're like and no matter what you can do or can't do. He wants to take you. He wants to fill you with himself. And he wants to use you to do the work of the kingdom.

*Tony Campolo is professor of sociology at Eastern College in St. Davids, Pennsylvania. He has authored nineteen books. Tony travels all over the world each year speaking at youth and missions-related conferences. Tony is also the founder and president of Evangelical Association for the Promotion of Education, an organization that sponsors education, medical, and economic development programs in Third-World countries as well as established ministries for "at risk" children in the inner city.*

2

# Igniting Volunteers to Become World Christians

*Jim Burns*

One of the most frequent questions I get asked by pastors from a host of different churches is, "How can I get my people excited about missions?" Let's face it, you can preach the most eloquent messages in the world on missions involvement but that is no guarantee that they will get involved in the cause. In fact, you can provide the best flip chart ever created on the missionary journeys of Paul and you can even bring in missionaries with the most elaborate slide show ever created but most people will still not respond. The key to igniting volunteers to become world Christians is found in one word: *experience*. Once people have been given a taste of what missions is all about, there will be no holding them back. It was definitely that way for my own journey toward a more global view of ministry and missions. Let me illustrate from my own life.

Several years ago I was visiting a school in Guayaquil, Ecuador, and there I met a little girl named Rebecca. I wish you could meet Rebecca too. She had the biggest, most beautiful brown eyes of anyone I had ever met. Her high cheekbones, long brown hair, and glorious smile would make any eye turn her way. Little Rebecca is eight years old and lives in one of the poorest slums on the planet. She is one of those kids you just want to pick up and hug. In fact, during the hour and a half I spent at her school, she held on to me. I let her climb on my back, we held hands; all through my journeys around her village, Rebecca never left my side.

Rebecca in Ecuador will never have the same opportunities my eight-year-old daughter Rebecca in Dana Point, California, will have, because Rebecca in Ecuador is pitifully poor. Her smile shows teeth that are already rotten. Her diet consists of one meal a day of rice flavored with onion and, if she's lucky, part of a potato. That's what she eats every day.

As Rebecca gets older, those beautiful brown eyes will dull and her energy will wane. Life will become more difficult. She will probably get sick, or pregnant in her teenage years, and by the time she is thirty years old, Rebecca will look very, very old and haggard.

When it came time for me to leave and say good-bye, little Rebecca ran alongside our vehicle. I rolled the window down to say one last good-bye and she screamed, "Jaime, tu eres mi hermano" ("Jimmy, you are my brother!"). My heart was broken! I left a little piece of it with a girl in a dirty slum in South America. I left Rebecca's village a changed person. Although I never went back to help her, I have never forgotten the words, the smells, the sights and sounds . . . and especially the need. That night in the comfort of my hotel room I re-read a parable of Jesus.

Then the King will say to those on his right, "Come, you who are blessed by my Father; take your inheritance, the kingdom prepared for you since the creation of the world. For I was hungry and you gave me something to eat, I was thirsty and you gave me something to drink, I was a stranger and you invited me in, I needed clothes and you clothed me, I was sick and you looked after me, I was in prison and you came to visit me." Then the righteous will answer him, "Lord, when did we see you hungry and feed you, or thirsty and give you something to drink? When did we see you a stranger and invite you in, or needing clothes and clothe you? When did we see you sick or in prison and go to visit you?"

The King will reply, "I tell you the truth, whatever you did for one of the least of these brothers of mine, you did for me." Then he will say to those on his left, "Depart from me, you who are cursed, into the eternal fire prepared for the devil and his angels. For I was hungry and you gave me nothing to eat, I was thirsty and you gave me nothing to drink, I was a stranger and you did not invite me in, I needed clothes and you did not clothe me, I was sick and in prison and you did not look after me."

They also will answer, "Lord, when did we see you hungry or thirsty or a stranger or needing clothes or sick or in prison, and did not help you?" He also will reply, "I tell you the truth, whatever you did not do for one of the least of these, you did not do for me." [Matt. 25:34–35]

I was motivated to examine my commitment to missions by the experience of the day and the powerful words of Jesus. He was saying to me, "Jim, when you serve poor and powerless people like Rebecca, you serve me." Obviously, we can't take everyone in our congregation to a Third-World country. However, *experience* is the main ingredient for igniting volunteers to mission participation, and anything you do to give them a taste of short-term activities will start to kindle their flame for mission service.

Here's a bold statement I once heard, and I believe it is more true than we want to admit. If we really wanted to build a lifestyle of servanthood and global ministry we would eliminate Sunday schools and use the money and time for missions experience. If everyone in the church could participate in a missions experience each quarter you would have a more powerful impact in ministry as well as Christian lifestyle. Christianity would be relevant in their lives because it would be something that was being tested on a daily basis as opposed to a weekly spectator activity.

## Experience versus Spectators

Our society is an entertainment-oriented culture. Unfortunately many churches have taken on the same mindset. I've spoken in some of the largest churches across America and frankly some of them have become wonderful entertainment centers. They are creating an entire generation of Christian spectators. The consequence of such a false Christianity, however, is a loss of global perspective.

Researchers in the field of educational psychology tell us that we learn best by experiential learning. I am grateful for Edgar Dale's

"Cone of Experiential Learning" because it helps me understand how important it is to get people involved in missions beyond the spectator level. Dale states that the average person retains only 5 to 10 percent when he or she must learn through either verbal or written teaching styles. Yet, the church has continued to put a major emphasis on lecture and reading. Dale's thesis is that the more involvement there is in learning the more learning will take place. When people *experience* something they will retain over 80 percent of the content (see table 2.1).

### Table 2.1
### Cone of Experiential Learning
#### A person remembers:

|                          | After 3 hours | After 3 days |
|--------------------------|---------------|--------------|
| If he only **hears** it  | 70%           | 10%          |
| If he only **sees** it   | 72%           | 20%          |
| If he **sees** *and* **hears** it | 85%  | 60%          |
| If he **experiencs** it  | 85%           | 90%          |

There is simply nothing like experiencing something for making it stick in your mind. Once the impression is made, it will always be there to influence you for the rest of your life.

Gordon MacDonald, pastor of Grace Chapel in Lexington, Massachusetts, believes pastors should experience one cross-cultural mission trip a year to help give their congregation a better world perspective. Dr. David Hughes, at First Baptist Church, Winston-Salem, North Carolina, helps any member of his congregation to visit the mission field by providing up to half of the finances for the trip through a special missions fund. Whether the missions experience be visiting a widow's home, serving sandwiches at a soup kitchen, or spending a few weeks in Haiti, every congregation will be changed through first-hand experience.

## Servanthood versus Self-Serving

Our culture tells us to "Look out for number one" or to ask "What's in it for me?" However, the call to Christ is the call to serve. One of our primary tasks as Christian leaders is to help instill an attitude of servanthood within the hearts of our people. When Christians develop a lifestyle of servanthood they are imparting a ministry for life. The great missionary doctor Albert Schweitzer once said, "I don't know what your destiny will be, but one thing I know, the ones among you who will be really happy are those who have sought and found how to serve."

When you give people the opportunity to serve and minister, that's when you will see them become world impactors, and their own priorities will change as well. I discovered that when people become servants they lose their own personal petty problems. In essence, they gain a broader perspective about the real issues of life. I love the little plaque above a friend's stove, "I complained because I had no shoes, until I met a man who had no feet."

Jesus gave his disciples a powerful yet simple demonstration about what it means to serve others. It is found in John 13:

> Jesus . . . got up from the table, took off his outer robe, and tied a towel around himself. Then he poured water in a basin and began to wash the disciples' feet and to wipe them with the towel that was tied around him. [3–5 NRSV]

Notice that although Jesus was the disciples' Lord and Master, he took off his outer garment and tied a towel around his waist in order to serve them. This is a strange act for a teacher—then *or* now. It obviously had a profound effect on Peter, for we later read:

> He came to Simon Peter, who said to him, "Lord, are you going to wash my feet?" Jesus answered, "You do not know now what I am doing, but later you will understand." Peter said to him, "You will never wash my feet." Jesus answered, "Unless I wash you, you have no share with me." Simon Peter said to him, "Lord, not my feet only, but also my hands and my head!" [6–9]

After Jesus had washed all the disciples' feet he sat down to explain the demonstration:

> "Do you know what I have done to you?" he asked. "You call me Teacher and Lord—and you are right, for that is what I am. So if I, your Lord and Teacher, have washed your feet, you also ought to wash one another's feet. For I have set you an example, that you also should do as I have done to you. Very truly, I tell you, servants are not greater than their master, nor are messengers greater than the one who sent them. If you know these things, you are blessed if you do them." [12–17]

In this experience Jesus gave all of us a clear message: *serve others.*
Notice the promise he makes in his last statement: "If you know these
things, you are blessed if you do them." In other words, Jesus claims
that when you follow his example of servanthood you will be happy.

## The Great Paradox

This whole idea of becoming other-centered is a paradox. You
usually become unlovable when you seek love. Yet, when you give
love, you become loveable and happy. Self-centered people are un-
happy. Other-centered people are happy.

Perhaps an illustration will clarify this. In New York City a woman
had been moving from doctor to doctor describing her physical ailments. The doctors would give her a thorough examination and yet
could find nothing wrong with her. One wise old doctor examined
her and then talked with her about her ailments. He told her emphat-
ically that he had the answer to her dilemma. He wrote out on a prescription tablet, *"Do something nice for someone else every day for fourteen days in a row and come back and see me."* He said the prescription
would cost $150, but that it had a money-back guarantee.

The woman looked at the prescription. "You mean there's no med-
ication?" she asked. The doctor replied, "That advice is the best med-
ication in the world."

The woman tried the doctor's prescription. On that very evening
she baked some cookies and delivered them to the apartment of a
lonely senior citizen. The next day she helped another senior citizen
with some shopping. She volunteered at the church, ran errands,
wrote kind notes, gave phone calls of encouragement, and every day
chose to do something nice for someone else. Fourteen days later she
walked into the doctor's office a new person—healthier, happier,
and more content than she had been in years. She gave the doctor a
hug and said, "Thanks for placing some good old-fashioned common
sense on your prescription pad. I get your message loud and clear."

Too many people today are consumed with their own petty problems. They miss out on the joy of serving. It seems that one of the
major complaints in America is money; no one seems to have
enough. Many Americans can't seem to get past their financial wor-
ries. Yet it's a fact that the clothes you wear in one day cost about the
same as what the average Haitian or Ethiopian makes in a year!

Contrary to what some teach, a selfish lifestyle breeds unhappiness. Jesus was right when he said, "For whoever wants to save his life will lose it, but whoever loses his life for me will save it" (Luke 9:24).

## Take a Stand

You'll ignite volunteers to become a world Christians only when you have truly become one yourself.

> In the days of Ezekiel God said, "I looked for a man among them who would build up the wall and stand before me in the gap on behalf of the land, so I would not have to destroy it, but I found none!" [Ezek. 22:30 NIV]

God is still looking for men and women with a whole-hearted commitment to him. He is looking for men and women who will stand in the gap. One of the greatest enemies in the Christian church today is apathy. To take a stand means to be willing to serve and follow the example of Christ, who was called the suffering servant in the Old Testament. If you take the time to historically review the major spiritual revivals and renewals that have taken place you will find that almost all of them have come from young people. Perhaps it is because older folks are more set in their ways. Young people, when motivated properly, are more willing to take a stand—even to the point of death.

For example, three years ago fifteen children sang hymns and prayed for freedom in Trimisorra, Romania, on the front steps of a sixteenth-century church. They were protesting the evil leadership of Nicolae Ceausescu and the lack of freedom in their beautiful country. As they sang and prayed, others watched and still others sat inside the church to support and pray for them. Ceausescu's secret police also stood by in silence. Then the secret police received the word and the word was "gun the children down." They raised their AK–47s and murdered every child. Those kids were truly martyrs.

Three years later, Romania is free. It is the end of one of the most wicked reigns of leadership ever known. Nicolae Ceausescu announced when he took over power, "Within twenty-five years, I will destroy Christmas and Easter." I am happy to say, Ceausescu was wrong!

# Preach the Gospel . . . and If Necessary Use Words

I believe that one of the grave sins of the church in years past was to separate the ministries of evangelism and social action. Nelson Bell, the great Christian statesman and missionary doctor to China, put it best when he said, "If you separate evangelism and social action, you only have half a gospel."[1]

In past generations, the theologically conservative church became uneasy with the liberals' desire for social action, so they backed away completely from social action and social justice. On the other hand, the liberal church became so caught up in not wanting to look like fundamentalists that they walked away from the core of the gospel, evangelism. People today must come to terms with the fact that social action and evangelism are inseparable.

Dietrich Bonhoeffer was once quoted as saying, "To allow the hungry man to remain hungry would be blasphemy against God and one's neighbor, for what is nearest to God is precisely the need of man's neighbor. It is the love of Christ which belongs as much to the hungry man as to myself. If the hungry man does not attain to faith, then the fault falls on those who refused him bread. To provide the hungry man with bread is to prepare the way for the coming of grace."[2]

The apostle John wrote toward the end of his life, "Dear children, let us not love with words or tongue but with actions and in truth" (1 John 3:18 NIV). I think Saint Francis of Assisi had that verse in mind when he said, "Preach the Gospel . . . and if necessary use words."

## Conclusion

I will never forget a chapel experience I had my first year at a Christian college. One day a missionary speaker stood on the platform and I pulled out the latest issue of *Time* magazine to read. I admit it; I didn't give the gentleman a chance. Yet his opening line was thought provoking. He stood in front of the podium, pointed his finger at the crowd and yelled, "You are the only Jesus somebody knows."

I smiled and went on thumbing through the magazine when his second statement caught me off guard. He again yelled, "You are the only Jesus somebody knows," pointing his index finger at another person in the audience. He proceeded to repeat that one statement over and over again. On the tenth time, I looked up and he was pointing his finger right at me. I put the magazine down. I don't remember another word he said, but his opening sentence kept churning inside my brain.

In my life, he was right. I had the awesome privilege and responsibility of representing Jesus to many of my friends and family. They weren't attending a church and had never made a commitment to make Jesus Christ their Lord and Savior. They didn't read the Bible and they seldom, if ever, talked about the Christian faith. As if in a very still, small voice God spoke to me and reminded me, "You are the only Jesus somebody knows."

I was told once about an American soldier in Europe after World War II who walked into a doughnut shop and bought his breakfast. When he walked out of the shop he noticed a little boy with his nose pushed up against the window of the little bakery. No doubt the boy was one of the thousands of orphans left after the war.

The soldier walked halfway down the block, then abruptly turned around, went back into the same bakery, bought a dozen doughnuts, and handed the doughnuts to the little orphan boy who still had his nose pressed against the window. The little boy looked at the doughnuts, then looked at the man. He stared at the soldier intently and said, "Mister, are you God?" The soldier's act of kindness was an act of God in the eyes of the little boy.[3]

The call to Christ is the call to serve. The truly committed Christian often rises to positions of leadership. Did I say rises? The truth is that every Christian leader must stoop to positions of service. Radical Christianity leads to servanthood. Your job is to give the people around you the opportunity to serve and experience ministry. God's job is to break their heart with what breaks his heart.

*Jim Burns is president of the National Institute of Youth Ministry. Highly respected for his expertise in the area of youth ministry, family, and parenting issues, Jim is the author of over twenty-three books and speaks to thousands of young people across the nation each year.*

3

# Developing
# a Christian World View
# in Your Church

## Paul Borthwick

A member of the missions committee came to me two years ago with this question: "Why do we get such great involvement at our Christmas pageants but such dismal attendance at missions events?" I gave a few trite answers in immediate response, but his question got me thinking.

Was it because our presentations were shabby? Perhaps, but we had worked hard to see that they were well planned and well delivered.

Was it because our speakers were boring? Maybe, but we had hosted some of the top missions speakers in the country, and the turnout was still poor.

The chapter is adapted from "Overcoming Missions Malaise," an article that appeared in *Leadership* (Summer 1988): 88–94. Used by permission.

I finally realized that the focus of the two presentations was different. The Christmas pageant was a festive celebration of the gospel, culturally acceptable. The essence of cross-cultural missions is also the gospel, but in the form of cross-bearing unselfishness. Christmas pageants could satisfy those who came to receive; missions meetings were for those ready to give.

That evaluation forced me to realize that the task of building a "vision for world missions" in the local church is full of obstacles that demand unique solutions. We can respond, but we must be realistic. Here are four problems we have discovered—and four ways we're attempting to overcome them so that a Christian world view can be developed in our church.

## Problem 1: The Task Is So Big

People come to church for a variety of reasons. Some have genuine spiritual hunger that they come to satisfy. Others are coming to meet social as well as spiritual needs. Children and young people may come at the will of their parents. Hurting people come to be cared for. The motivations vary, although spiritual growth is at least one of the driving forces. It's safe to assume, however, that most do not come to church to get overwhelmed by statistics, needs, and guilt-producing overviews of the task before us.

Here we face our first obstacle—people don't want to be overwhelmed, but the realities of our world are overwhelming:

more than 5 billion people are now living on earth;

urban sprawls will soon (if they haven't already) exceed the populations of major countries (example: by the year 2000, experts predict that Mexico City will be home to 30 million, which will make it more populous than Canada or Australia);

more than 700 million people are bound by the fatalism of the karma of Hinduism;

more than 800 million give allegiance (sometimes fanatically) to the Allah of Islam;

one out of every five people on earth (over 1.1 billion) live in the People's Republic of China, and many of these without any knowledge of Jesus Christ;

greater needs than ever with respect to sickness, hunger, and poverty are prevalent.

And these statistics just scratch the surface. The number of "children of the streets" in some cities, added to the people carrying HIV, plus the people in our own country who are responding to non-Christian religions that have come to the United States ("New Age" Hinduism, the Black Muslim movement, or popularized Zen Buddhism) add up to one word: OVERLOAD!

A college group called recently to ask me to speak on being a "global intercessor." When I asked for more details on what they wanted, they explained, "We'd like you to teach us how to pray around the world."

When I explained that with more than two hundred nations, more than fifty thousand missionaries from North America, and thousands of Christian leaders all over the world, "praying around the world" would take all day every day, they were overwhelmed. We settled on "Praying with a Concern for the World" as my topic.

Since 1983, "missions" has been a part of my job description. I'm supposed to know and manage some of these facts and reduce them to understandable terms for our church. It's overwhelming. And I know that if it's overwhelming for me, the person in the pew will shun a world vision simply because the task is mind-boggling, and "what difference could my puny efforts make in the total picture?"

I don't believe people are apathetic as much as they feel the subject is simply too large for them to respond to. So they shy away from it, believing their own worlds are the only places where they can make a difference. They need help in developing their vision.

## Our Response: Manageability

World Vision once printed a poster that summed up the need for a manageable response. The poster had a picture in the upper corner of a mass of suffering humanity. A question followed: "How do you help feed 1 billion hungry people?" In the opposite, lower corner was a picture of one malnourished child. The caption: "One at a time."

Missiologists may be able to think in terms of thousands, millions, and billions, but I can't. My capacity is closer to "one at a time" thinking.

Our church supports more than seventy missionaries. Even that overwhelms some attenders who want to know more about missions. So, rather than encouraging them to get to know "the missions family," we encourage people to adopt one missionary family. We give them prayer packets (with recent newsletters, a picture, and a one-page summary of the missionary's work, as well as a pre-addressed, stamped aerogram to get them started corresponding) to help them begin a relationship with one of our mission families.

In addition, we're trying other ideas (some original, but most borrowed from other churches we know about through our affiliation with the organization Advancing Churches in Missions Commitment [P.O. Box ACMC, Wheaton, IL 60189]) to make missions meaningful, practical, and manageable:

> encouraging the adoption of one "people group" for prayer and research (the folks at the U.S. Center for World Mission [1605 East Elizabeth, Pasadena, CA 91104] are most helpful here);
>
> making the *Frontier Fellowship Global Prayer Digest* available for daily use (available from the U.S. Center for World Mission);
>
> inviting people to read *The Church Around the World* (Tyndale House Publishers, Box 220, Wheaton, IL 60189) on a monthly basis;
>
> creating our own missions calendar so that people are encouraged to pray for two to four missionaries each month;
>
> focusing on one missionary per month in our "Hall of Missions" display and one missionary per week in our pastoral prayer;
>
> recommending starter books on missions—for instance, missions theology: *The Great Omission* (Robertson McQuilkin); missions biography: *Shadow of the Almighty* (Elisabeth Elliot); general vision: *A Mind for Missions* or *How to Be a World-Class Christian* (Paul Borthwick);
>
> getting people involved in service projects in nearby areas as well as in other cultures in our region and the world;
>
> challenging people not to overcommit themselves by promising to pray for and support dozens of missionaries but rather to make only those commitments they can manage.

It is our genuine desire to stir people to action and involvement in world missions, but we recognize our responsibility to prevent them from being paralyzed by the enormous size of the task.

## Problem 2: Zealots Poison Attitudes

While most members may be overwhelmed by the task of missions, there are often a few in the church who catch a vision for world evangelization and become totally devoted. They are on fire for missions, and they expect the entire church to join them in their zeal.

Some may respond, "I wish I had one person like that in my congregation" or "If I didn't have such people, there would be no missions emphasis at my church."

Why, then, do I consider these people problems?

Missions zealots are assets to the overall program, but if their energies aren't directed, they can also be liabilities, so "on fire" that they consume the people they touch rather than enlighten them. Zealots can erroneously communicate the message that only the extremely committed (a term that may be synonymous with "fanatical" or "weird") can be involved in missions. Thus, they aggravate the problem of missions being perceived as only for the specialists rather than a church-wide challenge that involves every member.

We have had our share of missions zealots. I think of the woman who could quote so many statistics about world needs that we nicknamed her "The Grim Heaper" because of her propensity to induce guilt. Or the man who thought every Christian should be as concerned about the 16,750 unreached people groups as he was (and to question him was to bring your own salvation into question). Or the young person who had no tolerance for those who desired to expend any monies on the operation of our church because "the needs over there are so great."

All these people have ultimately served our missions programs effectively, but their zeal has been directed so that missions has become an inclusive activity rather than an exclusive one. They serve as great resources to developing the vision of others—if we act wisely.

## Our Response: Balance

The challenge for church leaders is to provide balance so that the enthusiasts keep growing and the uninvolved are invited to get started.

Jill came home from college totally committed to missions. She took time off from her schooling to travel the country, campus to campus, with a team of "missions challengers." She explained, "We go onto a campus, challenge students to get serious about God's call to missions, and then we deal with those who respond."

"What happens to those who fail to respond?" I asked.

Jill replied matter-of-factly, "We shake the dust off our feet and move on!"

"Aren't you thinking of being a missionary in North Africa with Muslim people?" I replied.

"Yes."

"Well," I said, "if you carry that philosophy of recruitment to North Africa, you'll have clean feet, but no one will be won to the Lord."

Jill had failed to make the connection between the patience she would need with Muslim people and the patience she needed with average Christians for whom a commitment to world missions was a new concept. Helping our zealots learn this patience is the most difficult part of the balancing act.

In practical terms, balance is best achieved when we're setting the example ourselves as leaders. If we can demonstrate patience and concern for the uninvolved, the enthusiastic ones are more likely to follow. I try to communicate to those who are on fire for missions that growth occurs best if they

> realize God has given them a unique ability and concern;
>
> realize they are a crucial part of God's *big* picture, but so are the missions-docile members of our church who need rousing;
>
> see themselves as motivators of others (I challenge them to warm others to their fire for missions rather than consume them);
>
> dedicate themselves to the patience, understanding, and vision needed to invite others to join them in fulfilling the Great Commission;
>
> recognize that many growing Christians are uninformed about missions or what it means to be a "world Christian," but that this is a result of lack of manageable information, not aggressive rebellion.

God has brought us many wonderful zealots for missions, and it's been a joy to grow with them. For Rick, balance has come as a result of working with junior-high young people. His enthusiasm for missions and service caused him to volunteer for youth ministry. He thought, *"If I can influence these kids, they will grow up thinking about missions service."*

Rick's goal has been achieved, but in a way different from what he expected. At first he pushed the junior-high boys to "get serious about God and commit to his purposes." We worked with Rick and encouraged him to challenge his students from a platform of relationships. There are now many young people who have been influenced by Rick in their understanding of and commitment to missions, but it has come as a result of his loving them and investing time in their lives.

Ann's zeal for missions service has been tempered by her leadership in a small group. She has been sensitized to the fact that not every Christian is ready at the same time. Gradually, she has been able to influence others by presenting a bigger view of God in their Bible study. In Ann's words, "I learned that exciting people about missions is like serving a meal—it's better to serve up just enough so that people can't wait until they eat again rather than stuffing them with the first serving so that they never want to see food again."

By working to help people balance their missions commitment, we're able to utilize the energies of missions enthusiasts to make missions an inclusive rather than an exclusive church vision.

## Problem 3: Missions Seems So Outdated

Another obstacle to developing the world Christian vision of others is their perception of missions as shabby and outdated. Sometimes this image is of our own making.

We requested and were granted space for a "Hall of Missions" outside our sanctuary several years ago. We hung flags, put up missions pictures, and assembled racks for prayer letters. It was adequate, but not attractive.

We let the Hall of Missions stand until the day Bob said, "Paul, the Hall of Missions is a good concept, but it looks like it needs to be dusted."

Bob is not anti-missions. As a matter of fact, he's supportive. He was simply being honest. Our display looked shabby.

Many of us have had similar experiences with missions presentations. Some of them need to be dusted. Franklin Graham wrote that as a young person, his impression was that missionaries were people who were "always out of style." We all know the stereotypes: out-of-focus slide shows with a predictable closing sunset shot; ill-prepared missionaries who really should not be preaching. Working to overcome the poor performances of the past, we find ourselves swimming upstream.

Mrs. Elton, a missions leader at a nearby church, told me recently, "We have solved the problem of poor attendance at our missions meetings. We used to identify upcoming mission speakers in our bulletin as 'Mr. So-and-so, missionary from XYZ Mission.' For those services, our attendance declined. So now we just say 'Mr. So-and-so will be speaking,' and we don't tell people who he is. Now our attendance is steady."

We are all working to repair the bad image that has labeled missions in the past, and, in so doing, mobilize others to get involved in the task.

## Our Response: Nothing Succeeds Like Success

We're trying to apply to missions the adage, "You never get a second chance to make a first impression." If we do finally get the opportunity to present a missions focus in a major church service, is the interview well rehearsed, is the projector in focus, is the material to be handed out reflective of the caliber of work we want to support? (Has the Hall of Missions been dusted?)

To help our missionaries, we produce an informational bulletin entitled *Doing Your Best at Grace Chapel*. In it, we outline our church's constituency, our expectations of them as speakers, and our plan for missions long-term. We get specific about our expectations: the length of time they're to speak, the clothing appropriate for a given meeting (and we provide a clothing allowance, in some cases), language that will needlessly alienate some of our people (using "men" when referring to both men and women).

Our missionaries have expressed gratitude for our candid assessment of our congregation's particular expectations. It helps them be culturally sensitive as they make the adjustment back to the United States.

One final lesson we're learning is that we must bring missions to the people. If people are going to see missions as part of their daily commitment to Christ, we must start where they live, even in church life.

Several years ago, we planned a missions conference. We made sure our church calendar was cleared for the conference week. Despite no competing committee meetings or choir practices, however, the conference attendance was still poor. Why?

Our cleared-out schedule backfired on us. Most people looked at the schedule and said, "Great, a week off!" The people who came were those who believed in missions already. We didn't touch those who knew nothing of missions.

For the past two years, we've changed our strategy. Instead of canceling regular group meetings, we have asked groups to host a missionary speaker or feature a missionary focus that week. The result has been outstanding. Although we would still like to see better attendance at our main conference sessions, we are seeing more people than ever exposed to missionaries and world needs. Consider these examples:

- Our single-parent support group wanted a speaker who could address both a missions topic and the needs of the attenders. One of our missionaries spoke to the group on "How God Uses Our Lives in the Midst of Our Brokenness." It was one of their best missions meetings ever.
- Our children's Sunday school leaders meet monthly for dinner and planning. We provided a missionary who spoke on "How to Make Missionaries *Real* to Your Students." It was a helpful evening for teachers who are trying to expand young children's views of the world.
- The community Bible study for women was reticent to allow us to make a missions presentation at their meeting because "many of our women are from other churches, and we don't want them to think we're forcing them to be involved in Grace Chapel activities." So we suggested a creative angle. At the close of their Tuesday meeting, we set up a phone call with two of our missionaries, one in Germany and the other in Haiti, both of whom previously had been small-group leaders in the Bible study and knew many of the women. We plugged the phone into the church's sound system, and the entire Bible study group "talked" with their friends who were now serving overseas. It was a great day for building missions interest in the Bible study.
- Several groups have adopted missionaries, while others have undertaken special financial projects. Close to 50 percent of our congregation gets exposed to some specific aspect of missions (in addition to the Sunday services) as a result of this decentral-

ization. In our former clear-calendar missions conference approach, we averaged only 10 to 20 percent throughout the week.

# Problem 4: It's So Easy to Give Up!

A friend in ministry wrote to me, "We tried developing a world vision in others; we tried making missions a priority. We were going to learn about other countries, expand our missions budget, and add some missionaries to our support list, but we got waylaid by 'other things.' A few deaths in the church family, a hassle over the Christmas program, and a staff resignation was all it took for our missions plans to be tabled for another year. I simply don't know how to make the 'over there' aspect of missions real to our people."

Missiologist J. Herbert Kane writes in *Wanted: World Christians,* "After the second or third generation, Christianity tends to take on cultural overtones, and soon its members begin to take their heritage for granted and lose all desire to share their faith with friends and neighbors. The churches turn inward on themselves, and soon their chief preoccupation is their own survival, not the salvation of the world" (p. 205).

How can we get our people interested in being world Christians when the needs nearby distract our attention? With all the pressure to be more community minded or to attend to pressing needs at hand, it's easy to give up on missions emphasis.

## *Our Response: Endurance*

Needs close to home will demand our attention, but we cannot let these needs diminish our overall commitment to see the gospel communicated to all people. We need bifocal vision, a balance of being concerned close to home (near-sightedness) and committed to world evangelization (far-sightedness). Persistence is important in developing such vision.

Tom came to our church with a desire to see us involved with international students. At that time only two or three families were interested. Tom persevered. Three years later, our church hosted the annual Thanksgiving conference for International Students, Inc. Over two hundred students attended, representing more than forty countries. Almost seventy Grace Chapel families hosted students. Tom's endurance is bearing fruit.

Endurance is the willingness to persevere even when there's little apparent interest. In 1978, we started sending out young people on summer mission service teams. At that time, only a few of our adults supported the idea. Fifteen summers later, the endurance has paid off: more than five hundred young people, collegians, single people, and couples have gone out on some seventy-five service teams. Our teams currently include adults, and we have sent people as young as twelve and as old as sixty-nine into foreign cultures and needy areas of the United States. Summer missions service teams have been our greatest asset for building missions excitement and commitment at the grassroots.

## Seeing Both Far and Near

International missions cannot be our solitary focus. If it is, we'll cease to exercise the day-to-day love toward each other that identifies us as the community of Christ. A commitment to missions does not imply a one-sided view of ministry, but rather the near-sighted/far-sighted balance. Missionary statesman Osward J. Smith said, "The light that shines the farthest shines the brightest close to home."

Jack is a bright light. He's committed to evangelism and, as a layman, leads our training program for evangelism. He's an active Christian witness in his place of work, but he is solidly committed to world evangelization as well. He makes sure his Sunday school class knows and prays for missionaries; he involves others in listening to missionary station HCJB (Quito, Ecuador) over short-wave radio; he's using his international business travel opportunities to learn more about God's work in other parts of the world. Jack has a growing bifocal vision.

Our missions events may never match our attendance for concerts, Christmas pageants, or Easter services, but we can get our congregations aware of missions. When I'm prone to give up, I remember the changes in people's lives as they've opened their eyes to God's world and their hearts to his service. I remember . . .

Bryan and Janet, who have opened themselves to full-time ministry in a "second career" phase of their lives because they've been surrounded by missions-minded friends;

Marion, who chose to go to Haiti to serve meals rather than enjoy
    retirement in a rocking chair;
Debbie and Norm, who got started learning about India by invit-
    ing an Indian family to their home for their first taste of pizza;
Nathan, who, at age three, doesn't have a broad world vision, but
    is learning to say "Africa" with excitement;
Bob, who has worked out his own international vision by leading
    our service teams and by serving in our functions for interna-
    tional students.

All of these are lay people who have enlarged their vision for the
world through the perseverance of some and the prayers of others.
These—and the dozens of others being changed by a greater view of
God and his world—encourage us to face the problems and move toward being a missions-minded congregation.

*Paul Borthwick is missions pastor at Grace Chapel in Lexington, Mas-
sachusetts. He has written numerous books in the field of missions and has
been a national leader in helping church volunteers get involved in short-
term missions. He is a popular mission conference speaker at camps and
Christian colleges.*

# 4

# Focusing on Priorities: People versus Projects

## *Michael Anthony*

Each year I bring a team of students from Biola University on a short-term missions project over Easter vacation. Some years we have done famine relief in Haiti and other years we have done a vacation Bible school in the remote jungles of Belize. The past few years have been spent doing a variety of projects in rural areas of the Dominican Republic. When I first began doing these trips I used to think the goal was to get the students to the field and home again without losing any of them. As I gained experience I began to expand my purposes. Some trips have been very people-oriented (VBS or orphanage ministry) and other trips have been more project-oriented (building a kitchen at a Child Evangelism Fellowship [C.E.F.] camp or digging an irrigation canal for Food for the Hungry).

## Not All Projects Are Created Equal

About ten years ago I brought a team of college students to the Dominican Republic to dig an irrigation canal for the relief agency Food for the Hungry. It is an excellent organization doing valuable work in rural areas of developing countries. When I first heard about their need I got excited because I knew that our entire team would participate on the project together. Back in the sterile confines of my office it seemed like the ideal project for a ten-day trip. After all, anyone could dig with a shovel and it wouldn't take a great deal of advanced training. However, once we got to the field I quickly came to the realization that a mutiny could occur on locations other than a ship!

The ditch was to be several miles long across land exposed to the heat of the Caribbean sun. We were one of several teams that would join in on the project over the course of several months. Our group neither began the project nor saw it to its completion. We added to the length of the canal but little else. The front of the line stood in a water-filled bog about a foot deep. Each person began scooping water and mud until the person at the back of the line was eight feet below the surface in a trench two feet wide. We began digging at 8:00 a.m. and ended at 4:30 p.m. The heat and humidity were oppressive and within days our team was shrinking in size due to heat exhaustion, dehydration, fatigue, and mild dysentery.

We finally completed our allotment of trench and rejoiced to see our goal accomplished. My joy was tempered when I returned home and realized we had spent our entire trip holding on to the end of a shovel in a deep Caribbean trench. We had neither experienced the culture nor met any nationals. Worse, when I returned a year later I discovered the trench had been filled in and never used. I learned some valuable lessons from that trip: not all projects are created equal; not all projects are necessary; as volunteers, we had the right to get something of value from the short-term mission experience; some projects are better left to nationals. In this case, we could have paid a national worker a few dollars a day to dig the ditch and he could have fed his family for months. It was poor use of the nearly one thousand dollars it took to get each of us there.

## Find a Balance in Your Objective

Some activities provide substantial assistance to the local community. Other projects may actually serve your needs better than those of the people you go to help. It isn't wrong for you to expect to get something out of the trip. I have friends who lead short-term trips today and spend the entire time building a wall or adding a roof to a building. When they return I ask them how they liked getting to know the people of that culture. They look at me with amazement and say, "Who had time to meet nationals? We were too busy building a community center." Such a trip left out an essential missions ingredient: people!

I'm leaving with a group of twenty-five students next month to go back to the Dominican Republic. This time there will be no ditch. Instead we will have a variety of projects that take into consideration the needs of the local community in which we live *and* our own needs as North American visitors. When we arrive we will spend two to three days working with children at a local school. We'll conduct teacher training seminars for local teachers and help construct some badly needed playground equipment. After that we will spend a day bringing some joy to a community of lepers that the world has neglected and forgotten. One day we will spend touring a children's hospital in downtown Santo Domingo. Another day will take us to a Haitian batte in the rural outskirts of town where malnourishment is rampant and infant mortality is astronomical. We'll visit a girls' prison and a boys' prison while sharing a program of hope and salvation in Christ. Toward the end of our trip we will drive up to the Haitian/Dominican border and spend a couple of days building and working with (not for) the local people. By the time the ten-day trip will be over the team will have experienced and observed ministry in a school, hospital, leprosarium, prison, rural batte, and inner city. We'll do evangelism, construction, and medical, education, and visitation ministries. It will benefit the people of the Dominican Republic and it will also meet my goal of a short-term missions team: to expose people to the broad variety of ministry opportunities on a foreign field.

The students who major in nursing will see how medical missions is done. Those who major in education will experience a small piece of educational missions. Those with a sociology major will see life in the institutions of a Third-World country; those who major in physical education will see athletics as a viable ministry opportunity.

Now when I return the team to the airport for their trip home there will be tears of farewell and departure. Students' hearts will be broken by what they have seen and experienced. Their mind will go back to the sick child in the dirty hospital ward, a child who had been abandoned in a trash can the week before. They'll reflect on the leper who put his arms around them and said, "Thank you for caring enough to come and visit me." My students will smile as they recall the three hundred screaming children who laughed at their VBS puppet show. How the children hugged them to show their love and the sparkle in their eyes when the candy was distributed. These college students will never be the same again!

# Some Pros and Cons of Construction Projects

## *Pros*

Some people will volunteer only for construction-type projects. Perhaps they are threatened by interpersonal relationships with people who do not speak their language. Some are skilled in a particular building trade and that skill is badly needed in a remote village. For example, I once brought a professional painter to a vocational training institute in the interior of Haiti. It was his first mission experience and he would never have signed up if his expertise wasn't needed.

For individuals who feel threatened by evangelism-type activities, the construction project is an appealing reason to go to the mission field. Electricians, carpenters, plumbers, painters, and mechanics are all badly needed on the mission field. It is a natural invitation for them. It allows them to feel needed and it can make a difference to have a professional builder on a construction site.

Another advantage of construction projects is that they are measurable. North Americans love to measure their progress. They need to look at something at the end of a day and see the results of their efforts. For example, a foundation was laid, walls were framed, a roof was completed. These are all measurable ways of demonstrating progress. When the team goes home, people can show photographs to their supporters to prove the value of their investment. It contributes to a sense of accomplishment and success.

A third reason for doing construction projects on a short-term mission trip is that they let just about anybody join in. After all, how much pre-trip training does it take to teach a volunteer how to nail a board or paint with a brush? Men and women, young and old can all do something to help at a work site. Even children can haul water for thirsty workers or help mix cement. Construction projects allow you to invite more people and they take less time to train volunteers.

## Cons

There are a number of disadvantages, however, for doing construction projects on a short-term mission trip. Construction projects can insulate you from getting out into the community and associating with the nationals. The entire trip can be spent hammering wood or painting a wall. There is nothing of eternal value in either activity. The wall will need to be repainted again and the roof will need to be reconstructed.

This mentality of insulation is what Samuel Melo (the author of chapter 10) describes as Delta Force Missions. Volunteers, feeling the need to conquer the task, throw themselves so fully into the project that they want nothing to do with anyone or anything that does not relate to accomplishing the task at hand. They want only to get the building done, take a photograph of the completed job for the sponsors back home, and then head for the airport home. Mission accomplished!

Along this line Mary Fisher writes, "There are times (on the mission field) when I just want to get on with the work, with the program, with the 'ministry.' It's so much easier than taking the time for relationships. But then the Lord reminds me that everything I do counts as nothing when my relationships are not in order. I remember my true calling as a Christian—a calling to reconciliation so that the fruit of the Spirit may be manifest in my life. Then the focus of ministry changes from task to relationships. . . ."[1]

Another disadvantage is the possibility of inexperienced volunteers getting hurt doing something they aren't trained to do. Most Third-World countries operate on 220 volts for electricity and that is no time to experiment on how to wire an electrical outlet! Two high-school students were recently killed in Tijuana, Mexico, when a hole they were digging caved in on them. Who would have thought you could get killed digging a hole on a weekend missions trip? The students simply didn't know the risks and didn't take the necessary precautions.

A third disadvantage is the cost that construction projects add to the trip. When the expenses of building materials are added into the trip budget it can make the difference between some people being able to go or not go. Some groups have overcome this problem by raising the costs of construction projects independent of the trip costs. A special offering or fund raiser can defray these costs. In fact, some people are more motivated to give and support a missions trip if something tangible like a hospital, an orphanage, or a church is built as a result. They will provide all of the costs for the project if the school, infirmary, church, or clinic is named after a loved one.

A final disadvantage is generally overlooked or downplayed but it is extremely important. This disadvantage relates to the dignity of the local community. When a North American group arrives and does all of the work on a building project it prevents local workers from gaining employment. Third-World countries have carpenters, stone cutters, ditch diggers, painters, plumbers, and electricians too. When we do the work we contribute to their unemployment. It is also poor stewardship of our money. Why should I spend three thousand dollars to send a twenty-five-year-old college student to dig a ditch when a local man could do the job just as well (probably much better) for three dollars a day and feed his family for a month by receiving employment? In essence, our missions trip can devastate the local economy. It is no wonder some communities have grown to despise North American Christianity.

Building projects should include money in the budget to hire local construction workers. The employment gives your volunteers an opportunity to meet nationals and your employment helps strengthen the local economy. As people from the community work on construction sites they develop a growing sense of pride and self-respect for their own community. It returns dignity to their lives and they will take better care of the final project if they made a personal investment in it. In addition, when you go to their church and do a program, they will be more receptive to your message if you have earned their respect by working alongside them.

Please don't misunderstand what I am saying. I am not saying that we should neglect building projects in developing countries. On the contrary, these projects are essential to the development of the Christian faith oversea. Nationals may be hesitant to go to a church but they will send their children to a village school, medical clinic, or community center. Many times it is the North American church that provides these buildings.

What I am saying is that as North Americans we must be wise stewards of the limited resources that God has given to us. Let's not do the work, but work alongside nationals. In areas where we bring an expertise that they do not have, such as education, medicine, counseling, or building trades, then we should invest those skills. However, if they have the ability to build buildings themselves but lack the financial resources to do it, it is wiser for us to do what we do best and allow them to do what they can do best. It makes no sense to bring a medical doctor from the U.S. and have him or her lay concrete for a dormitory in Honduras.

# Some Pros and Cons of Working Exclusively with People

## Pros

It is exciting to see a needy person, whether a child or an elderly adult, come to faith in Christ. Few joys in the Christian life measure up to that thrill. Projects that involve your volunteers with nationals will produce bonds that will last for years to come. Ministry activities such as evangelism, teaching, or counseling involve the volunteer in the lives of others. That rich bond will last far longer and be more meaningful than a material possession or a project based on manual labor.

A second reason to involve yourself in the lives of those in the community is so you can fulfill the Great Commission, which requires personal involvement in the lives of others. I once had a professor who said, "There are only two things which will last for eternity: people and the Word of God. Your job as ministers is to put those two together." People last for eternity, so mission activities that are designed around people will produce results that can last for eternity.

A third reason is that getting involved with people will help your group understand the culture better. They will gain a deeper understanding of the values, traditions, and customs of the host country. Your volunteers will gain a deeper appreciation for those of different ethnic origins that can't be developed in a work or a construction project. They will also come to appreciate the work of full-time missionaries who come from North America and the challenges that they face when they try to do ministry in a foreign country.

## Cons

One reason why it is difficult to work with people on the mission field is that effective interpersonal ministry requires some knowledge of the language and the ability to work within the constraints of a foreign culture. This is not easy to do and can't be accomplished in a mere six-week training program.

A second reason for the challenge of working with people is due to our human nature. Regardless of culture or national origin, all people have personal prejudices, egos, and personalities. When our character traits conflict with the character traits of others from a foreign country there can be significant problems. These interpersonal conflicts can be difficult to manage and even more difficult to resolve. Dealing with people is always a challenge but add a different culture and a lack of understanding about getting things done in a foreign country and you have the ingredients for a potential skirmish that even the United Nations would find difficult to resolve.

## Conclusion

Over the years of visiting the foreign field with short-term teams of volunteers I have discovered that missions trips that are designed exclusively around a construction project will appeal to some and discourage others. Likewise, projects focused purely on personal evangelism, teaching, or counseling have a natural draw for some but will distract others.

The Bible says that we are each given a unique gift when we become part of God's family. Each gift plays an important role and *together* those gifts help meet the needs of a local body of Christ. No one gift is more important than another and each complements the other. Mission trips that take advantage of the diversity of skills and talents of each team member help ensure a more meaningful trip for all.

My preference is to put together a mission trip that provides a balance between work projects and interpersonal activities. The key is to know what you want to get out of your trip. If you have a group of retired builders you certainly would do well to organize a mission trip that uses their building expertise. I doubt many of them would sign up to direct games for Vacation Bible School. However, a group of high-school students will not be qualified to construct a hospital in the countryside. To be most effective a mission trip should take into consideration both the needs and the abilities of the volunteers as well as the needs of those to whom you minister.

Understand that it is all right for you to expect to get something from the trip as a group. You are called to give but in the process of giving you should also be willing to receive. When your volunteers return from their short-term experience they will be more effective members on the church missions committee, they will develop contentment by appreciating their own living conditions more, they will appreciate people from foreign cultures because they will know how difficult it is to function in a different culture. The list of what you can receive as individuals and as a church-sponsored group is almost endless. The key to getting the most out of your short-term experience is to know what you want to accomplish and to find a balance between working with projects and working with people.

*Michael Anthony is associate professor of Christian education at Talbot Seminary at Biola University. He is an avid world traveler and loves to spend his vacations leading short-term groups on the mission field. He has ministered in over a dozen countries around the world.*

# Selecting and Screening Volunteers for Service

## Judy TenElshof

Secular business has long known that putting the right person in the right job is a difficult thing to do. The consequences of putting the wrong person in a critical position can devastate the productivity of a corporation. Imagine what it would be like if you were greeted at the gate of Disneyland by an employee who was irritable and obnoxious!

In the same way, ministry must seek to put the right person in the right job. That's why churches put their friendliest people at the front door on Sunday morning to greet visitors. Visitors get a better introduction to the church; this experience in turn makes them want to come back.

Jesus understood the importance of placing the right man in the right job. He did not select his disciples without giving significant thought and prayer to the matter. In fact, we read in Luke 6 that he spent the entire night in prayer before selecting his disciples. Apparently he had a multitude of individuals following him and he had to make some decisions about who qualified for leadership and who did not. Screening these individuals was critical to the success of his ministry venture.

During the entire process of recruitment and training, screening should be taking place. Some recruits may be too self-focused, like Judas, who had selfish motives for serving. Others, like Peter, may require great investments of personal energy and attention. Then too, the problem may not be with the individuals themselves but with a pushy parent, as in the example of James' and John's mother. She wanted them in places of honor on either side of Jesus, places for which her sons had not been prepared. Jesus understood the need for proper selection and screening of volunteer workers.

Participating in a short-term mission experience will almost certainly require one to sacrifice personal desires for what is best overall. The sacrifice may be as large as giving your life or as small as not being as clean as you would like. For example, when I was recently in the Philippines on a short-term mission experience, it was so hot and humid that make-up and good hair days were impossible. We ran out of water for baths and out of gas for cooking. The only liquid we could safely drink was Coke. Several members of the team got incredibly sick. Was I prepared? Yes. Enough? No! If it weren't for the fact that I knew it was God's work I was doing, I probably would have lost sight of my purpose for being there.

The purpose of this chapter is to help the leader of a short-term mission experience understand how to select and screen volunteers for service. Without proper selection and screening, the effectiveness of the experience may be compromised and the trip itself may be wasted. Just one wrong person on a team can undermine and devastate the entire venture. What follows are some practical guidelines to help you select and screen volunteers.

## The Selection and Screening Process

The first step in the selection process is for those who will be sponsoring and leading the trip to meet and assess the realities of the experience. How long will the trip be? How primitive are the living conditions? What level of personal and spiritual maturity should the team members possess? What specific ministry or construction skills will be needed? Before the church even communicates the missions trip, some advanced selection criteria need to be established.

The next step in the process should be to develop a short-term mission application packet. This helps ensure some degree of objectivity on the part of those who will make the selection. It also forces the participants to think through and examine their motives for involvement. Here is a list of some of the items that should be included in your application packet:

1. *General information*
   name
   address
   phone
   citizenship
   date of birth
   education
   employment
   gender
   marital status
2. *Family background*
   description of family of origin
   any history of abuse as a child
   any experience with drugs, alcohol, cults
   divorce or family tensions
3. *Spiritual development*
   Christian growth experience
   description of testimony
   history of church involvement
   ministry experience
   special training received
   spiritual gifts
4. *Health issues*
   ability to cope with stress
   allergies
   disabilities
   emotional stability
   history of illnesses
   medications
   physical limitations

5. *Reference letters from*
   pastor who has known the applicant for several years
   teacher or civic group leader
   friend or someone who has known the applicant for several
       years
6. *Detailed description of the mission trip*
   This description should be as complete as possible so people
   can screen themselves. Include:
   location
   length of stay
   focus of mission
   what kind of applicant should apply (age, gender, marital sta-
       tus, special skills or abilities needed)

The next step in the selection and screening process should be a
personal interview with the candidate and the leadership team of the
mission trip. In some cases it might also be helpful to invite a representative of the church board to join the committee. Some larger
churches also have the candidates meet with the church's missions
committee. This allows the members of the missions committee an
opportunity to know who is going on the various trips that the
church is sponsoring and to get acquainted with each of the individuals participating in short-term trips.

This process can be quite time-consuming but it is an important
part of the selection and screening process. The purpose of the interview is to determine whether or not the candidate matches the information on his or her application. You also want to use this time to
explore issues that may have arisen as a result of reading the application materials.

The interview should begin with building some rapport by sharing
something of yourself or something you may have in common with
the applicant. You will want to create a safe and secure atmosphere
in which a deeper level of interaction can take place. The questions
should be open-ended and include a combination of things you may
need to know about all of the applicants and information you need
from this particular applicant. Some sample questions are

What made you decide to apply for this mission trip?
Tell me about some of your cross-cultural experiences.

Describe your relationship with God.
How does your family feel about your going on this trip?
How do you resolve difficulties with others?
How would this experience strengthen your relationship with the
Lord?
What is your greatest concern about going on this trip?

The application and the personal interview for the most part
screen for personal reasons that the applicant may not be ready to go
on a short-term mission experience. Some of those reasons could be

Skills and abilities do not match those needed on this particular
trip
References reflect a lack of maturity
An uncooperative spirit or lack of respect for authority
A personal disability that can't be compensated for on this trip
Being sent by parents

Most organizations stop screening once the applicant has submitted his or her application and passed the personal interview. One of
the reasons they quit so early is because the interviews aren't completed until just before the trip is to begin. This also doesn't allow for
much team cohesion to take place. A team lacking cohesion will be
self-focused and unable to accomplish the mission with maximum
effectiveness. Dave Hicks, the North American director of Operation
Mobilization, says, "The number one problem in missionary work
today is broken or strained relationships. When our relationships are
strong, enormous resources are released to accomplish the work of
God. When relationships are strained, the energy of the Holy Spirit
working through us is drained away."[1]

## The Use of Profiles and Tests

The use of personality profiles and psychological tests can be somewhat controversial to some churches. If you value them but your
church does not support their use, then don't force the issue. You can
glean a lot of the same information through personal interviews and
watching the candidate respond in interpersonal relationships.

Several tests could be helpful in discovering personality traits, conflict styles, or family background. The longer a team is going to be on the field the more in-depth the testing should be. For very short-term missions (less than one month), tests such as the Taylor-Johnson Temperament Analysis, Family History Analysis, or the Thomas-Kilmann Conflict Mode Instrument could be used. If the mission is longer than one month, more in-depth testing such as the Myers Briggs Inventory or the Minnesota Multiphasic Personality Inventory could be given. The disadvantage of the latter test, however, is that it requires specific training in its use and interpretation. Most of the others require only minimal or moderate amounts of preparation and training to learn how to use them properly. You might want to consider asking a professional counselor from your church, if you have one, to join the selection team.

Testing candidates has a threefold purpose:

1. For individuals to know and accept their own traits and styles in relationships.
2. For each member to trust others on the team with both their strengths and weaknesses.
3. For each member to accept team members' differences and to love, confront, and forgive each other as needed.

Stephen C. Hawthorne, a leader of several short-term teams in Asia and the Middle East, says, "A short-term experience is a great way to discover how valuable and yet how dependent you really are. Jesus said that the sower and reaper can rejoice together. Don't miss out on the joy of partnership."[2]

## Time Frame for the Selection and Screening Process

As you can see from the number of things to be done in the selection and screening process, it will require some time for it to be done right. Don't try to shorten the process by deleting elements of what have been presented. Each of the steps is critical to the entire process.

I believe the ideal amount of time you will need to select and screen your volunteers for a short-term mission experience is approximately six months. There needs to be time for team members to learn how their personality differences are beneficial or detrimental to the effectiveness of the whole team. Safety and security with each other need to be built so each member can share honestly and openly his or her opinions and feelings. If conflict arises, there needs to be enough time to gently and compassionately confront so members can seek forgiveness and reestablish trust.

Team members also need time to get to know their leaders. Stephen T. Hoke, vice president for training at Church Resource Ministries, says, "All too many short-term workers neglect building relationships with their leaders."[3] Romans 13:1 says we need to be subject to those in authority over us. And Hebrews 13:7 says we need to imitate the faith of those who lead us. This means we need to know our leaders and spend time with them. Building team relationships is difficult work and will stretch every team member. It is important to allow enough time for the process to take place.

## Conclusion

It is not easy to put together a team for short-term missions. Anyone can form a group but it takes real skill to turn that group into a team. This process should include a thorough screening of the applicant through a formal application, personal interview, applicable testing, and individual discovery.

The time that you spend becoming a team before you depart for the short-term assignment will pay tremendous dividends in the future. The process itself should be a growing experience for both leaders and team members, one that will result in truly saying "mission accomplished."

*Judy TenElshof is an instructor of Christian education and marriage and family ministry at Talbot School of Theology. She maintains a private counseling practice and is currently pursuing a Ph.D. in marriage and family therapy from Fuller Seminary. She has participated on several short-term mission trips through her home church, First Evangelical Free Church of Fullerton.*

Part 2

# Mission Experiences Abroad

This section is designed to help you deal with the practical issues associated with bringing volunteers to a foreign field for a short-term experience. Two of the most important issues you'll face are fundraising and gaining the cooperation of the church board. Each is a critical and essential activity before the missions team departs.

In addition, since we live in an increasingly litigious society, a church should do everything it can to protect itself from litigation in the event of an unforeseen accident. Additional chapters related to selecting a sponsoring organization to join with, understanding the field representative's perspective, and the importance of training and preparation are all practical areas for your consideration.

This section is full of insights from seasoned experts that will be of tremendous value to you as you make preparations for your departure.

# Financing Your Mission Experience

## Kim Hurst and Chris Eaton

Church finance and missions committees are beginning to learn one of the mysteries about raising money for short-term mission involvement. You can make the most heart-wrenching appeals for money from the pulpit for an overseas building project, a missionary in need, or the general missions budget of the church yet never raise a dime. But if one of your church members signs up to go to the mission field on a short-term mission trip, an abundance of money appears. Why is this true? What is the secret? The answer has to do with why every short-term mission team—whether it is comprised of flat-broke students or multimillionaires—should make fundraising a part of its pre-field preparation.

## Why Do Fundraising: A Tale of Two Churches

"I'm afraid we're going to have to cancel our short-term mission trip to the Dominican Republic. We just can't seem to get a team together; money's just too tight in this economically depressed region."

I sighed silently as I listened to the pastor on the other end of the phone line. With just a few months left to go, he was scrubbing his church's mission team. Did he know how much the Dominican church members were looking forward to this team, a team that would have helped build the village's new school? Did he understand that even though the building might well be constructed by some other team in the future, his congregation would now miss the opportunity to form relationships that would last into eternity?

And then I wondered, did he know that just across town—in the very same economically depressed region—I was working with a team that had thirteen members who had all been able to finance their travel to the Caribbean and had raised an additional three thousand dollars in project costs? How is it that one church had seen nothing but obstacles, where another had seen only opportunity?

The second church knew the secret! The secret is this: there are four reasons to conduct fundraising for your short-term mission and only one of those reasons is the need to raise funds! Those organizations that capitalize on the other three will find a church that becomes committed to the success of its short-term missions endeavors.

## Four Reasons for Fundraising

The four reasons for fundraising include raising the money needed, increasing the awareness level of friends and family about the missions trip, building spirit and cohesiveness among the team members, and helping the team members exercise their faith muscles.

*Fundraising raises money.* In a chapter on fundraising, it is probably wise to begin with the obvious. A good reason to conduct fundraising is to finance the mission trip. Some of the people who benefit most from participation on a team, and have the most to offer, are those who cannot afford to pay the cost of participation. It is an unfortunate fact that many people in our churches would be interested in joining a short-term mission experience if money weren't a factor.

*Fundraising raises awareness.* This is where fundraising becomes more than a means to an end. Consider the following illustration:

Linda was a new believer when she was asked to join her church's short-term mission trip to Costa Rica. She looked forward to the opportunities she would have to work on a worthwhile project, to meet Christians from another culture, and to share her newfound faith.

But she knew her salary as a telephone receptionist at a construction firm was not sufficient to raise the necessary funds.

So, with the holy boldness that is characteristic of new believers, she began to explain her vacation plans to all her work associates. She went so far as to send one of her fundraising letters to the owner of her company's major supplier, a man she knew was not a church-goer. Not only did this man write a check to cover all of her costs, but also he kicked in some extra funds for anyone else on the team who might need the help. But perhaps more importantly, he became genuinely interested in Linda's trip.

When she returned, she found he was more than enthusiastic to see her pictures, to hear her stories, to learn how God had used that short-term mission trip.

And it is not just the unchurched whose awareness is increased. We're fond of using a riddle to illustrate the point when we speak to groups on this subject:

> **Question:** If twenty people from your church are planning to travel to another culture to participate on a short-term mission, how many people are on the team?
> **Answer:** The whole church!

That's because when fundraising is done well, the entire church becomes involved in the plans of the short-term missionaries. Miami Shores Presbyterian Church has come up with a clever way to in-volve church members in the short-term missionaries' experience. Instead of asking for donations, team members sell shares in the short-term mission. Shareholders buy stock in the trip and then re-ceive dividends in the form of postcards from the destination city and a souvenir brought back from the field. Most importantly, share-holders are invited to an annual meeting, usually a dinner, in which they hear and see reports of how the short-term mission affects the lives and the faith of the missionaries and their hosts. By becoming shareholders, these donors literally have stock in the success of that short-term mission.

*Fundraising builds team spirit and cohesiveness.* Whether you ask those who send short-termers or those who receive them, all will agree that the success of a trip is measured by how well everyone works together. Short-term missionaries may be part of a team sent by a church or a college, or they may go individually to the field and join with others there. Either way, teamwork is the key to an effective mission trip. For this reason, we spend a great deal of our pre-field preparation time building good teamwork skills among our short-termers.

One of our most effective tools for accomplishing this is to have the group work together to raise funds. In this way, fundraising becomes an equalizer, something requiring the efforts of all the team, those who have discretionary funds and those without.

We break the price of the mission trip into two parts: the team member cost and the project cost. For example, a trip from Los Angeles to a Navajo community in Arizona will cost each participant approximately $250 for transportation, food, and lodging. For many people, $250 is relatively affordable, and chances are most team members would be able to write a personal check. In addition, the team pledges to raise an additional $2,000 for building supplies—a cost that is raised jointly by all members of the team.

Another example is a team traveling from Boston to Guatemala to build a school. The per person cost will be quite high for airfare alone, so many team members may need to raise funds for the per person cost. In addition, the team joins together to raise additional funds for the school building.

The same process applies even when there are no project costs per se involved in a mission. Often short-termers travel to the mission field to help with evangelization or to pitch in at a mission station that uses existing buildings. Nevertheless, the team works together to raise funds to be donated to the host community or missionary. We need to remember that hosting short-term missionaries can be a burden to the hosts; at the very least, it takes them away from their normal activities. We learn a tremendous amount by participation in the day-to-day life of our hosts, so it's good to consider the work that you do, or the money that you donate, as the tuition you pay for a valuable education!

*Fundraising exercises faith muscles.* Someone has said that if financing your trip isn't a faith-building experience for all involved, perhaps your sights are set too low!

One mission agency I know of must believe this to be true. One of their career missionaries is a person I have known for years, long before he was ever interested in full-time Christian service (an interest, incidentally, that was conceived on a short-term mission trip). I happen to know that before his present career, he had earned several advanced degrees, had worked as an attorney and an educator, and was responsible for managing his family's considerable fortune. Nevertheless, when the call came, he answered and is now serving in Latin America.

His mission was delighted to have him apply. But not because he'd have no trouble coming up with his monthly support. As a matter of fact, they told him to give his tithes and offerings elsewhere; he was to live as all their other missionaries do, on the prayer and donations of loving supporters.

He confided in me that this was perhaps the most difficult thing he was ever asked to do! All his life he was used to paying his own way, even donating generously to others. But asking for support! This was something new. It didn't come easy for him, but in time, as God provided the needed resources, he began to learn of God's abiding faithfulness. This same faithfulness would keep him on the mission field once he arrived at his assignment.

He has been on the field now for a couple of years. Each month he writes letters to his supporters, and each month he relies on God to provide his needs through the donations of others. He has become convinced of the wisdom of his mission. He has seen God's faithfulness in ways he was never able to witness firsthand until he became dependent on fundraising. Building spiritual muscles is a lot like building physical muscles. You need to exercise and allow your body to go through a little stress—in essence, to step out and let God reveal his abilities. Each time you do, your faith muscles will grow a little stronger.

## Ideas for Raising Money

As we have already said, money can be raised individually and as a group. The most effective way we know to raise individual funds is to write a letter for distribution to friends, co-workers, family members, and church members. Those who are hired by organizations to raise funds professionally will tell you that people are not stingy so much as suspicious.

Nameless, faceless institutions are not likely to receive many contributions, but the person you've already learned to trust will. Potential donors are happy to have the opportunity to invest in someone they know personally or an endeavor they care about.

Since many people who participate in short-term missions do so as part of a team, and since many team members seek donations from the same pool of donors—for instance, a local church—it is unwise to work from a sample fundraising letter. The last thing a donor wants to read is four copies of the same letter, with four different signatures!

Nevertheless, it is a good idea to make sure all fundraising letters contain certain information. The guidance in this chapter is reprinted from our book *Vacations with a Purpose,* a resource that has been used successfully by scores of short-termers.

*Sending letters.* One of the best ways to raise funds is by personally asking people to support you in the mission experience. Many team members have told us that even though they were initially put off by the idea of sending support letters, it turned out to be one of the best aspects of the whole adventure.

There are three types of letters that team members might send. Discuss with the team members their fundraising plan and help them decide which type(s) of letter would be most appropriate:

1. *Letter sent out by the team member requesting funds for his or her trip.*

2. *Letter sent out requesting funds for the project.* Perhaps team members will decide to pay for their own trip but wish to ask for donations for the project itself. In this case, team members will explain in the letter that they are paying their own costs, but are asking friends to join in contributing towards the project.

3. *Letter requesting prayer, but no money.* Even if you do not need any funds, we would encourage you to have team members include others in their mission trip. One great way is by inviting people to join with them in praying for the endeavor.

*Guidelines for writing your letters.* Team members who are raising funds for their own participation may consider sending letters to friends, business associates, relatives, and others. The fundraising letters should include the following:

1. *Information about the country/culture they are going to.* Include a brief description of the area and things such as per capita income, literacy rate, population.

2. *Information on the sending organization and the hosting organization.* The sending organization is the church or ministry that is planning the trip. The hosting group is the mission agency and/or national church you are working with.

3. *Description of what the team will be doing.* Here is a good time to include why the team is doing this particular project. For example, if you are building a rural clinic, why is that a need in the community?

4. *The cost of the trip.*

5. *Why that person wants to be involved in this trip.* Remembering to be brief, list the reasons for going on this trip that you feel strongest about. However, while your letter may mention your desire to become more globally aware and develop a deeper faith, your readers are more likely to donate money to your support of an actual project or activity.

6. *How they would like the reader to be involved.* In the letter you need to address why you are asking the reader to contribute financially. Let's go back to the project example mentioned in item 3. If you are going with this team, then you are asking the reader to assist in supporting this endeavor by contributing to the expenses you incur by going. This need not be a long "sales pitch," but rather a simple request.

7. *Clear instructions on how the reader is to respond:*

Who to make check payable to (checks should not be made payable to the team member if the person wishes the donation to be tax-deductible)
Where to mail the check
When you need the money
Whether you are requesting prayer or financial assistance or both

8. *The team member should compose his or her own letter.* People will prefer to read a personalized letter as opposed to a form letter that is sent by everyone on the team.

9. *Keep it brief!* The first page will probably be read. Not much more than that will be read by the average person receiving the letter.

## Raising Funds as a Group

Raising money as a group involves a few different considerations. Several suggestions for raising funds are listed. You undoubtedly have ideas of your own. In addition, your public library or church library may have information on the subject. Keep a detailed record of the ideas you use and how successful they are. This record will help in the planning for future teams.

*Fun runs.* One large urban church has raised more than thirty-five thousand dollars in scholarships and project costs for four years by sponsoring a 10K run/5K walk held each year in the spring. The event attracts people of all ages from throughout the church congregation who enjoy the chance to participate in the festivities. Funds are raised by those who seek sponsors for their participation and by charging an entry fee to those more serious runners who like running in this offi-cially-timed race. This annual event now has the entire congregation involved in the idea and excitement of short-term missions.

*Work days.* In another group, participants ask people to sponsor them for their work in a community project. The participant pro-vides eight hours of labor to an organization like Habitat for Human-ity or at the home of an elderly or disabled neighbor. Again, in addi-tion to funds raised, participants have the chance to share their enthusiasm for the upcoming trip!

*Food fast.* On an individual basis, team members and other sup-porters can skip one meal a week for a certain number of weeks and give the amount they would normally spend on the food toward the project.

*Activities.* Plan an event and use a part of the price of each ticket as a donation toward the project. Another option is to contact busi-ness owners or social clubs and ask if they will consider your group in their plans for events already scheduled. For example, contact a large department store and ask if it will donate some of the proceeds from the annual spring fashion show. Thanks in part to the in-creased visibility of celebrities working for various causes, busi-nesses seem more willing to become financially involved in issues of global concern.

*Auction.* A church in New England conducted an auction for its young adult ministry's summer mission trip. In this event, people of-fered services they were willing to donate to be auctioned off. The services ran from "cleaning out your refrigerator" to "a gourmet meal for four." After two weeks of soliciting services from the group, the auctioning began. This event raised over three thousand dollars for the team!

*Shareholders.* This method, described earlier in the chapter, involves selling stock in the short-term mission trip. Shareholders receive dividends and attend an annual meeting. This method raises awareness as well as funds.

*Department-store inventory.* Many large department stores take stock of their entire inventory once or twice a year. This is an enormous task, requiring lots of employee hours and little skill. Groups can offer to participate in inventory—which usually involves getting your group to work all night long for one or two nights. The department store makes a donation to your group for the equivalent of several dollars per hour for each person who worked. Short-term missionaries and their friends and family can all pitch in for an effective fundraiser.

*A booth at the fair.* Many communities across the country have at least one carnival-type event per year in which civic groups host food booths, carnival rides, games, and crafts. Contact your local Chamber of Commerce to find out how your church could host a booth to raise funds for missions. (Note: Some larger churches have their own carnivals and raise quite a bit of money.)

## The Leader's Role During Fundraising

As a group prepares to take a short-term mission trip, the group leader or overseer should stay abreast of each team members' efforts to raise funds. Following are some guidelines for the group leader:

1. *Review all fundraising ideas* **before** *they are implemented.* By doing this you help to insure that nothing is going on that may compromise the integrity of your short-term mission program. Also, you may be able to add some valuable input into the implementation of an idea to insure its success.

2. *Regularly monitor how each team member's finances are coming in.* Establish deadlines and keep to them. Some people may put things off, a circumstance that can be complicated if you have airline bills to pay! By monitoring progress, you will be better able to encourage those who need it and affirm those who are doing well.

3. *Run the funds through the church. Do not run donations through your own account or through the accounts of individual team members.* In many situations, funds given toward short-term mission participation are tax-deductible. Check with the treasurer of the church to see

if this is the case and how he or she wants you to handle collection and distribution of the funds for the trip. Chapter 8 has more to say about this important topic as well.

4. *Bring the entire group into the fundraising endeavor.* The short-term mission experience should be owned by the group or church as a whole. If the entire congregation is a part of the fundraising, they will be interested and enthusiastic about your team's experience. As individual team members share their enthusiasm, more people become involved through prayer and support. In turn, the awareness and concern for missionaries and the broader church family grows far beyond the team itself. Since much of the support for these teams will come from unchurched friends and colleagues, including others in fundraising provides team members with great opportunities to share their faith and their concern for the world once they've returned.

5. *Encourage those not raising their team cost to raise project funds through support letters.* There will be those who feel uncomfortable sending out letters asking people to contribute to them personally, but they may not feel uncomfortable asking people to contribute to a school building or for clinic supplies.

6. *Let team members know from the start exactly what the costs are and what they are responsible for.* One good way to do this is to spell out the details and expectations in writing and give them a copy at the first orientation meeting.

## Objections to Fundraising

Over the many years that we have been leading short-term mission trips we have heard a lot of objections about raising money. A sampling of some of these objections will help prepare for what may lay ahead:

*Objection 1: I'm scared to death to try and raise money.* I recall a conversation I once had with a member of my church who was very interested in taking a short-term mission trip. She seemed like a good candidate, so I was anxious to have her apply. Unfortunately, she never did. She later told me that she didn't have the money in her own account and would never "be caught dead panhandling money from friends and loved ones."

Attitudes like that are not uncommon. Many people have a strong and deep-seated fear of fundraising. A successful fundraiser will tell you that the biggest obstacle to raising the money you need is your own fear of asking. If you truly believe that what you are doing is worthwhile, if you honestly feel that the donations you are seeking are going to be put to good use, then your uneasiness is unfounded.

Any person who prepares to raise money for a short-term mission trip needs to be armed with a few facts. First of all, if your mission is well-planned and if you are making the trip at the request of the host missionary or community, then that receiver *needs* you. The host needs you in the same way he or she needs money. Many missionaries or other hosts put off certain projects until a short-term team is available to help in the ministry. Your presence is as important— sometimes more so—as your money. If you were collecting money to send directly to a ministry you felt good about, you would probably do so with great confidence. You ought to have that same confidence in asking people to help send you to the field.

Secondly, research conducted by James Engel and Jerry Jones and reported in *Baby Boomers and the Future of World Missions* shows that among baby boomers—the largest segment of the population—financial contributions to missions, personal involvement in mission and ministry, and global awareness all increased significantly among those who had participated in a short-term mission experience. When you take a short-term mission trip, you are in effect beginning a process that will make you a more effective global Christian!

Even when armed with self-confidence and the knowledge that your short-term mission endeavor is a worthwhile cause, you may still have a few concerns. We have listed the most frequent comments we hear when it comes to fundraising.

*Objection 2: Wouldn't it just be cheaper to send the money?* The answer to this concern is always, "What money?" The truth is, short-term mission funds don't generally come from church mission budgets. There is usually no reservoir of funds that gets earmarked for short-term missions at the expense of something else. Short-term mission funds usually come from vacation savings or from the donations of family and co-workers who would not normally give to church-related activities.

Additionally, an investment in short-term missions is an investment in the development of a future world Christian; the money donated now is likely to multiply in years to come as the short-termer becomes a mission supporter.

Finally, short-term missions are all about relationships: the relationships between Christians of different cultures, the relationships among team members, the relationship between Christians and God as the short-termer becomes a more mature believer. A donation sent directly to the mission field will not have the same impact as a short-term mission trip in developing these relationships.

*Objection 3: I don't want to ask people to pay for my vacation.* A properly run short-term mission trip is no vacation! Although it has many of the components of a good vacation—adventure, new environments to explore, new friends—it is a valuable tool used by the church to spread the gospel and to meet needs. If you suspect your trip is going to be a vacation, you are either in for a surprise, or you have chosen a trip that will not be as effective as it could be for the cause of the gospel.

*Objection 4: People won't be interested in my trip.* Nothing could be further from the truth! They may not be interested in a two-hour slide show after your return. . . but chances are most people are fascinated that you have chosen to use your vacation time for such an endeavor. When I worked at a large law firm I found that my non-Christian co-workers were curious about my plans. I found that discussing upcoming short-term mission trips was an effective way to share my faith with them. Upon my return, I could always count on a good crowd to see my pictures and hear about the various aspects of my experience, even the "churchy stuff." Many non-Christians who are wary of giving their money to organizations are happy to make tax-deductible contributions to friends, especially when they see in pictures exactly how their money was spent.

*Objection 5: We're in a recession.* Many nonprofit organizations will tell you that giving sometimes increases in tough times. Perhaps its because people realize that if they're feeling a pinch, someone else is feeling a squeeze. A poor economy is no reason to think you will not be able to fund the trip.

## Conclusion

Fundraising can and should be an integral part of your short-term mission experience. By raising funds you raise awareness, build team spirit, and build faith. Fundraising is one of the best ways to let others know your plans and include them in your experience. So don't be intimidated by a fear of fundraising! Your short-term mission trip is a worthwhile endeavor; the more people you can include, the greater the benefit!

*Kim Hurst is the director of missions at the Crystal Cathedral in Garden Grove, California. Chris Eaton is president of Bridge Builders, Inc., an organization that pairs North American churches with churches overseas in partnership for community development. They are co-authors of* Vacations with a Purpose: A Planning Handbook for Your Short-Term Missions Team, *published by David C. Cook.*

7

# Cooperating with Church Leaders

## *Ken Garland*

Virtually everything a youth leader does with students in programming is done with certain risks. Most of the time, misgivings about a
missions activity for students on the part of church leadership involve concerns over the risks involved for the students as well as the
adult leaders of the activity. In this chapter we will try to enable the
reader to secure the support and the cooperation of church leadership for planned missions activities with students.

## Gaining Approval from the Leaders Involved

Many of us have been through the frustrating experience of securing the approval, support, and cooperation of multiple boards, committees, and members of the pastoral staff for activities only to find
that as we are ready to carry out the activity, some other leadership

group has created a difficulty because it was not involved in the planning stages.

The approval grid differs depending upon how your church governs itself, and it goes without saying that you should be aware of which governing boards and committees have some control over the activities you plan and carry out. Generally there are three levels of church leadership involved in getting approval for your missions activity.

## The Senior Pastor

In my experience, getting the approval and cooperation of the senior pastor has always been the first and most important step in gaining church support for any activity. Bill Stewart and Bill Yeager have noted that while the senior pastor may not be involved in the actual missions ministry, as the chief executive officer of the church he is held accountable by the church board and congregation with regard to all the ministries and activities of the church. Without his prior approval of your missions activity proposal, securing the support of other church leaders will be difficult if not impossible.[1]

## The Church Board

Once the approval of the senior pastor has been obtained, in most situations the next step is to get the support of the church board (usually the board of elders or the board of deacons). These people have been chosen by the congregation to provide oversight for all the ministries of the church including your missions experience. They have a right to expect you to give them full information about your proposed missions activity so that they can make an informed decision regarding their support.

Requesting their support may come from the senior pastor or perhaps directly from the staff member overseeing the trip. In some cases, the board may request that the staff member appear at the next board meeting so that they can have the opportunity to ask questions. It is essential that board members be kept informed about the essentials of the trip. Nothing can weaken your support with the board more than for them to get a call from an irate member of the congregation about an element of your trip that you neglected to tell them about. Be forthright with them from the beginning.

## The Church Missions Committee

In most churches a committee has oversight of the church's involvement in missions. Often this group is chaired by a member of the church board and is accountable to the board for its work. This group also has a right to be fully informed about your proposed missions activity. Once it lends you approval, it often is in a position to provide some funding from the missions budget to help defray some of the costs of the activity.

What you are planning to do at the church or through a parachurch organization regarding mission involvement should have input and support from the missions committee. If the committee is heavily supporting its denomination's mission activities and you are going through a parachurch organization, it is important that you communicate with the committee even though its support may be less enthusiastic.

# What Do These Leaders Need from Me?

Other chapters in this book give you information regarding the vision and planning that must go into preparing yourself and your volunteers for a successful mission experience. It needs only to be said here that the leaders mentioned are entitled to see a complete mission activity proposal in writing from you and your staff.

This proposal should include all the relevant information you have gleaned in researching this proposed activity. The amount and kind of information to be included will vary with the type of experience you are planning and the forms of governance used by your church, but Paul Borthwick's items to be included are well worth consideration:

Your goals and objectives for conducting the activity
With whom you will be working on the field
Your leadership team
An accurate analysis of the financial costs
A plan for raising the money if it is not a budgeted activity
Criteria for selecting people for the activity
Your plan for training the team
A careful analysis of the risks involved in taking a group where you
    plan to go.[2]

Obviously, all this means that you must begin the process of securing the cooperation of church leaders long before the planned dates of the missions activity. Communicating all this effectively to the pastor, board, and missions committee of your church will take time and the decisions regarding their support may be slow in coming. Borthwick says, "The amount of time required to plan a mission trip varies, but it is wise to consider planning anywhere from eight to twelve months in advance."[3] In most cases, after each level of leadership has read your proposal, each will have some specific questions that will need to be answered fully and carefully before final approval is secured.

Remember that these leaders have been selected by the congregation to provide wise direction to church ministries. Many of the congregation who chose these leaders, and some of these leaders themselves, are parents of students in your group who may be involved in the activity. They are concerned for issues related to fair selection of team members, adequate and mature adult leadership of the team (for those trips which involve minors), financial accountability of team leaders, and the safety and security of the team as they travel and minister. These concerns will be even greater if this is the first time you or someone in your church has planned a mission activity.

Ridge Burns suggests that, even before developing this proposal, you spend considerable time developing your own mission statement for what you want to do with your students. Burns says, "Before sharing your vision with your pastor, mission committee or Christian education committee, develop a short mission statement that you will be able to use as a basis for your discussion."[4] This mission statement should include two important components: the vision for the experience as it involves the volunteers and the specific objectives that you would like to see accomplished during the activity.

## How Should I Approach These Leaders?

The first step in developing your proposal involves doing your homework well. If this is the first experience of this kind for you, be sure to plan your missions event in cooperation with someone on the field you know and trust, or a professional agency that is experienced in providing the kind of event you are seeking. Chapter 9, "Selecting a Sponsoring Agency," can help you identify agencies that are skilled in providing the kind of experience you desire. These agencies are also able to give you the kind of information you'll need to gain the support of your church leadership. In some cases, a representative of one of these agencies may come to your church and help you make your proposal if necessary. Before approaching your pastor, board, or missions committee, make sure you have obtained the answers to as many potential questions as possible. You can be sure most of the questions you anticipate will be asked of you somewhere along the line, and the more answers you have, the more prepared you appear to be.

Working through experienced mission agencies and/or missionaries is crucial regardless of your level of personal experience. International travel can sometimes be difficult even under the best of circumstances, and in some parts of the world it is dangerous as well. You will serve yourself, your volunteers, and your church leadership well by planning your experience through agencies or missions leaders that are experienced in dealing with people in the part of the world to which you desire to travel.

If you are setting up the experience yourself, the proposal you develop for your church leaders should include the field to which you desire to go, the names of contact persons on that field who have agreed to work with your group, the types of insurance needed by the members of your group for the duration of the trip, the kinds of individual preparations needed by the members of your group to enable them to travel to your destination, and a list of the necessary inoculations for each group member. Remember that obtaining passports and visas for international travel can often take several months, so make sure you plan far enough ahead to allow time for each group member to secure his or her necessary travel documents.

Your proposal should also include information concerning where you will be housed while on the field, how you will make provisions for meals, how members of your group can be contacted in cases of emergency, and specific information concerning your travel plans (names of travel providers, a tentative itinerary, and any other information you can get regarding the experience you are planning). Most church leaders who have conducted several mission trips have learned that it is best to work through a respected and experienced travel agency when planning to travel outside the United States. These travel agencies can be a helpful source of information about the culture and background of the places you want to go as well as any expected dangers of traveling in that part of the world. They will also have the most current information regarding travel restrictions and advisories from the U.S. State Department.

Once you have done the research, the next step is to carefully and completely communicate your vision, mission statement, and proposal to the senior pastor, the governing board, and the mission committee of your church. Make sure you tell them everything that you know about the activity; do not withhold any information. Sometimes a leader will be tempted to keep from telling the pastor or board information concerning the risks or costs of an activity for fear that they may deny their approval for the activity. Resist that temptation! It is always better for them to know everything at the beginning rather than have them find out after the fact that you kept important information from them.

## Putting Feet on Leaders' Cooperation

All too often, once a church leader or leadership group has given support to a ministry proposal, they forget it in the press of other urgent church business. Once your pastor, board, and mission committee approve the trip it is important for them to help motivate the entire congregation to get behind the mission activity as well. There is a great deal that these leaders can do to lend cooperation and support to your activity and thus help make it even more successful. Burns states that the missions activity you have proposed really is a ministry of the entire church body, and everyone in the church should be encouraged to get involved where they can.[5]

Here are a few suggestions of ways in which the leadership of the church can "put some feet on their cooperation" with you in the missions activity.

*Have a commissioning service for the missions team.* In almost every church I have served over twenty years of youth ministry, the church conducts a commissioning service whenever a professional missionary goes to the field or returns to the field after furlough. The missionary speaks about his or her ministry upon returning to the field and church leaders gather at the platform and lay hands upon the missionary and pray for his or her fruitful ministry upon arrival at the field. Why shouldn't this same kind of emphasis be given to your student missions team on the Sunday before it leaves? Burns goes so far as to suggest that whenever possible, have the team leave that Sunday afternoon to give even more immediacy to the commissioning experience.[6]

*Collect special offerings and other resources.* Many times, some of the materials your team will need to conduct their ministry on the field can be collected from church members in the months and weeks before you go. Craft needs for a VBS program with children, clothing items to be distributed on the field, old eyeglasses, hearing aids, crutches, canes, and other medical supplies are just a few things that church leaders can encourage church members to contribute for the ministry. Then, the board and pastor can set aside a special time for an offering. This allows the members of the congregation an opportunity to support the financial needs of the student team before it goes to the field. There is no way to calculate the encouragement this gives to your students as they pray for a certain amount of money which is needed and then watch as God moves the congregation to meet that need in a special offering. I took student teams to Mexico for twelve years, and every year as we prayed for the money we needed, God moved, and every year the congregation contributed more than was needed in a special offering. There is no way to measure the amount of encouragement this kind of support gives to the students on your missions team. Kim Hurst and Chris Eaton talk about this important area in chapter 6, "Financing Your Mission Experience."

*Church leadership prayer partners.* There are a variety of ways to get the members of the congregation to give prayer support to your student missionary activity. For the purposes of this chapter, it is important to get the church leaders who have approved your activity to lend their prayer support. An adaptation of the prayer partner idea from Burns would be a great place to start.[7] Give to each church leader (senior pastor, board member, and mission committee member) a card with the name, address, and phone number of one of the adult sponsors or student participants on your missions team. Ask the church leader to call that team member to solicit any specific prayer requests that the church leader might pray for. This makes the support for the missions activity more personal for the church leaders who have approved your proposal and they are more likely to get involved with the student participants in the missions activity.

*Conduct a ministry report service.* As part of the proposal that you submit for approval, include a follow-up church service upon your mission team's return from the mission trip during which the team members will report to the congregation on their ministry. Getting the pastor, board, and missions committee to commit that time and to help put the service together will further insure their support and cooperation and will also further let the congregation know that the church leadership is fully supporting the mission event.

This service accomplishes two purposes. First, it lets your students know that the church and its leaders consider their experience important enough to commit a full service to them for a report. Second, it allows the church to see how much a group of teenagers who are committed to Christ can do when they are given a chance to minister.

The service itself should involve your students as much as is possible. The congregation would prefer to hear testimonies or interviews with the students as opposed to a sermon or report from the youth leader. Some suggestions:

1. Have one of the students who enjoys photography take slides of the trip. Make sure all the students have ample chances to be photographed as they are doing their part of the ministry. Their families will enjoy seeing them in action.
2. Maybe you could have members of your team dress in the clothing style of the people where you went. (Don't try this if your trip is to a primitive culture in an equatorial country where the natives wear no clothing!)
3. Role play some of the differences between American culture and the culture of the country you visited.
4. Share some of the worship music your group learned during their trip. Maybe you could have a musical student or two actually teach your congregation one or two of the songs you learned.
5. Have your volunteers keep a journal during the training for the trip and then during the trip itself. Ask some of them to read meaningful selections from their journals to the congregation.

## Conclusion

You want your short-term missions trip to be a memorable experience, but for the right reasons. If you follow the guidelines of this book, your experience will be memorable and the memories will be happy and good ones. Failure to plan and communicate effectively will likely cause your church leaders to deny you the privilege of having the experience. But in the event that you are allowed to proceed, failure to plan and communicate effectively will cause problems that will make your trip memorable, but the memories could be painful and frightening. Remember, you want the volunteers who take this trip to be willing to go on another one in the future, and you want them to encourage others to take a similar trip the next time, so make sure you're prepared.

*Ken Garland is chairman of the department of Christian education at Biola University/Talbot Seminary in La Mirada, California. Ken has been a full-time youth pastor for over twenty years and currently serves as a consultant to churches in areas related to youth ministry. He has published articles in* **Youthworker** *and the* Religious Education Journal.

# Legal and Liability Issues

## Dennis Kasper

In an increasingly litigious society, churches cannot ignore the risks associated with their operations. Short-term mission projects are certainly not exempt from these concerns. The risks are, however, reasonably quantifiable and with careful planning can be significantly minimized. In a short-term mission project, a church has two major areas of responsibility: supervision of the program itself, and the conduct of the participants in the program.

The church's first responsibility is to operate the mission program in a manner that does not negligently or intentionally cause harm to the participants and that complies with all applicable laws. This means that the church must use care in designing and administering the program so as to avoid reasonable risks of harm to the participants. In addition, the church must be sensitive to its legal obligations to those church employees who will be involved in the program. Finally, the church must be careful to comply with the laws that directly govern the activity. Among these may be the U.S. tax laws, immigration laws, and customs regulations.

The church's second major responsibility concerns the conduct of the participants themselves. This can involve providing adequate supervision so that the participants do not cause each other harm and taking care to be certain that they do not cause harm to others, especially those whom they are serving.

# Responsibilities for Supervision of the Program

## Liability for the Program

In order to limit liability, the mission program must be carefully planned. Trips should be planned by individuals who are well informed about the risks of the particular itinerary and are professionally capable of designing the program in a manner that minimizes those risks. If the church does not have such individuals on its staff, it should consider either sending the short-term mission participants through a reputable program or obtaining the services of a mission consultant.

Remember, if the program is being administered by the church itself, the leaders, whether they are employees of the church or volunteers, are agents of the church and the church will be responsible for their conduct.

Those who are providing leadership to the mission team should be carefully selected and trained. Increasingly, the courts are allowing claims against churches on the basis of negligent selection, supervision, and retention as a basis for liability. This means that even if the church would not otherwise have been liable for the illegal or harmful conduct of one of its agents, negligence in its selection or supervision of the person will make the church liable on that basis.

With this in mind, it is wise for churches to obtain background information on all participants in the leadership of any program, both paid and volunteer. An application form is the best initial source of this information. The application form should include a request for references and should ask for information about the person's prior experience in operating a program of the type to be conducted on the mission. References should also be checked carefully. Depending upon the nature of the trip, additional efforts may be necessary to insure the proper selection of the leadership.

Where minors are participating in the program, the application form should also include background information regarding the supervisor's prior experience with minors and specifically ask whether or not the person has been convicted of a crime involving child abuse. In addition, it is often wise to obtain fingerprints. In many states the authorities are more than happy to run fingerprints through their criminal justice network and determine whether or not a potential applicant for leadership has a record involving child abuse.

In addition to a thorough background check, each applicant for leadership should be carefully interviewed. The interview should be designed to evaluate the individual's skills as well as his or her maturity and ability to handle the responsibility associated with the assignment. Whenever possible, the interview team should include individuals who are familiar with the specific demands of the trip being planned. It is also helpful if the interview team includes at least one person who is trained in the mental health field. Refer to chapter 5 for more specific information about the selection and recruitment process.

Some churches have considered using psychological tests as a part of the selection process. Psychological tests can be valuable when they are administered by professionals and properly scored and interpreted. The tests may be of increasing importance depending upon the length of the mission trip and the responsibilities that the individual directing the trip is undertaking. In some parts of the world the ability to think on one's feet and handle high-stress situations is extremely important.

However, most psychological tests were not designed to be used as employment screening tools. In addition, because the tests often collect a great deal of private data in order to achieve their results, they are coming under increasing scrutiny by the courts. In some cases the administration of such tests to employees is governed by the Americans with Disabilities Act as well. In order to avoid the risks associated with the use of such tests, a church planning to use these types of screening tools should consult with its attorneys before doing so. In addition, if they are used, tests should be administered, scored, and interpreted only by competent professionals. Chapter 5 can provide additional information on this topic.

To the extent that the data to be collected in a psychological test can be directly related to the type of assignment the employee will have, the basis and justification for use of the test, and its value, will be increased.

Finally, a written record should be made of the selection efforts so that if a dispute ever arises the church will be in a position to demonstrate the steps it took in its selection process.

Once individuals are selected to provide leadership to a mission trip, those individuals should be thoroughly and carefully trained. That training should include aspects of planning for the mission trip itself, cultural issues, and crisis-management techniques. Chapter 11 has specific details on training.

It is important for those administering a program to be familiar with the details necessary to carry out the program; careful and thoughtful planning also should be given to possible risks associated with the program and the steps to be taken to deal with those risks. Not the least of these risks, in some parts of the world, are terrorist attacks and kidnapping.

Churches planning trips to such parts of the world should have well-developed crisis management plans. The leaders of the church mission trip should be familiar with contingency policies and be prepared to implement the crisis management plans as soon as it becomes necessary.

If the trip is to be conducted by an outside agency, the church should inquire about the agency's crisis management plans before selecting the agency. The agency should have a plan, and the church should be comfortable with the strategy it uses.

Where minors are involved in the program it is also necessary for the church to have a clear policy governing the conduct of the counselors and supervisors. Leaders of short-term trips should also be thoroughly trained in dealing with minors of the particular age in question.

Specific rules of conduct should focus, among other things, on the relationships between supervisors and minors. Those rules should limit the number of students per supervisor. The rules should also address gender relationships, including whether individuals of one gender should supervise students of the opposite gender.

Specific policies regarding keeping track of minors should also be included. Depending upon the nature of the trip, each minor should be the primary responsibility of at least one adult.

The training of the supervisors should include basic skills in communication with young people. The training should also explore with the supervisor the responsibilities for handling confidential information in a counseling setting and the duty to disclose information to parents when it is necessary or relevant.

Depending upon the state in which the church is located, the individuals conducting the program in which minors participate may also be subject to child abuse reporting laws. If they are, the training should include an understanding of how those laws work and the responsibilities for reporting child abuse.

## Employer Relations Issues

If those operating the program or participating in the program are paid employees of the church, the church must be certain that it complies with all applicable labor and employment laws. The church should pay particular attention to the applicability of wage and hour laws. In addition, depending upon the state in which the church is based, workers' compensation laws may be applicable overseas. The standard workers' compensation insurance coverage that the church has, however, may not extend to activities overseas.

Finally, in this area, the church should be sensitive to the fact that federal civil rights statutes, including the laws prohibiting sexual harassment, have been extended to protect U.S. citizens who are employed by U.S. employers anywhere in the world. The church should be clear with its employees that its policies governing these matters extend to the mission trip.

## Regulatory and Tax Issues

In planning a short-term mission, the church should be certain that it complies with the regulatory laws that relate to the mission project itself. The most obvious of these are those associated with U.S. and foreign immigration and customs matters. Appropriate travel documents including visas should be obtained. Appropriate planning should be given to customs regulations that might affect not only items that individuals bring back to the United States, but also items that are taken on the trip.

Particular attention should be paid to the fact that in certain parts of the world the United States government restricts or prohibits U.S.

citizens' travel and the delivery of goods. The failure to give careful consideration to these types of restrictions can result in the church leadership and the leadership of the mission project being subjected not only to civil liability but also to criminal liability.

The federal tax laws may also have an impact on the conduct of a short-term mission project. Typically, tax laws affect the project in one of two ways. The first has to do with the manner in which funds are raised for the project itself. The second has to do with the use of those funds overseas.

Although churches themselves are tax-exempt entities and, with few exceptions, are entitled to raise funds that are deductible to the donors, under federal tax law, donors may not take a contribution deduction for money they contribute to individuals. Where the church simply acts as a conduit for funds that are intended by the donor to go to a particular individual, the donor is *not* entitled to the deduction.

This rule can be of particular concern to churches in short-term mission projects where the participants are required to raise their own support. Where the participant raises the funds necessary to cover the costs of the trip, and the donor expressly designates funds to be used by the church for the benefit of the individual participant, there is significant risk that the contribution will not qualify as a tax deduction. In order for a contribution to be deductible, the church must exercise complete charitable control over the funds and must have the freedom to use the money as it sees fit.

If the participant in the program is required to raise funds for the church as a part of his or her participation in the program, rather than raising funds to cover the cost of his or her trip, the tax deduction will be preserved. This may appear to be a fine distinction, but it is a critical one from the IRS's point of view. If a church has any question about this it should consult with its tax counsel to be certain that it conducts the program properly.

In addition to concerns about funds that are raised for the program itself, there are federal tax limitations on what charitable organizations can do with the funds which they raise. Strict rules govern the transfer of charitable funds to organizations or entities overseas. The rules are less restrictive if the funds are used to purchase goods to be distributed or are used in connection with the charitable activity. In any case, however, if funds are to be taken overseas, or if goods are to be purchased with the funds to be taken overseas, the use of the funds and the items purchased must be consistent with the charitable purposes of the church. Again, any questions in this area should be resolved through consultation with competent tax counsel. The price for failure to observe these laws may be severe: the misuse of charitable funds can jeopardize the tax-exempt status of the church.

Finally, the use of charitable dollars to pay bribes or ransoms presents serious risks to the tax-exempt status of the church and may also violate other federal civil and criminal laws. Churches considering the payment of bribes or ransoms should consult with competent legal counsel before doing so.

## Responsibility for the Conduct of the Participants in the Program

The church is responsible not only for the conduct of the program itself, but also for some of the acts of the participants in the program. This responsibility falls into essentially three categories: responsibility associated with ensuring that participants do not harm each other; responsibility to ensure that participants do not harm others; and, to the extent services are provided by the missionaries, responsibility for the performance of those services.

The first concern, the responsibility to ensure that participants do not harm each other, can be dealt with largely by providing adequate supervision. It is essential that there be sufficient leaders to protect the individuals from themselves. This is particularly true where children are involved in the program.

Of perhaps greater concern is the responsibility for the conduct of the program and the provision of services to others. This can be of particular importance if the services include professional efforts. Where professional services are to be rendered (a medical mission, teaching, or perhaps, even, construction), it is important for the church to be familiar with the local laws and customs with regard to those services. If potential legal liability does exist, the church must be certain that the professionals provide services that are consistent with the standard of care in their field. It may also be possible to purchase insurance to limit the risk.

Similarly, if those on the mission project are going to be building structures or doing other similar work, the church must be certain that all local ordinances, such as building codes and permits, are observed. Obviously, this may not be possible in many Third-World countries but reasonable decision making should be exercised.

## Additional Steps to Limit Liability

A church can do a variety of additional things to limit exposure to liability. The planning, training, and supervision, described in this and in other chapters of this book, are certainly significant. In addition, however, exploring the purchase of insurance coverage is also useful. The church's general liability policy may not cover the trip, particularly if it is outside the United States. However, single-event coverage is often available, and the premiums may not be unreasonable.

In addition, employees of the church are generally covered by the workers' compensation provisions of the law in the state in which they live. Special rules sometimes apply, however, when the individuals engage in an activity on behalf of the church outside of the state, or more importantly, the country. Churches that send individuals on mission trips outside their state or out of the country should check with their workers' compensation insurance carrier to be certain that they have coverage.

In some states, workers' compensation insurance coverage is also available for volunteers. In evaluating the exposure to risk in a particular operation, it may be more cost-effective to purchase workers' compensation coverage for the volunteers participating in the mission trip than to try to insure them in some other way.

Liability release forms are also possible tools to limit liability. The purpose of the liability release form is to ask the participant to release the church from liability for any negligence it may commit in the operation of the program. The enforceability of these types of forms is limited, but some courts have upheld them where the activity is of a voluntary nature and involves significant risk. Mission trips to certain parts of the world might well fit this definition, particularly to the extent that participants in the program are volunteers rather than employees.

The liability release form, in order to be effective, must be carefully drafted (see the sample form in this chapter). The courts have held that the risks must be fully disclosed and must be expressly waived. In addition, in order for the form to be adequate in some states it is necessary for the waiver to include not only the participant but also his or her heirs and dependents. Also, courts in some states have held that these waivers may be entered into on behalf of minors or children by their parents or guardians. However, a church should not rely on this form as necessarily effective in its home state. If these forms are to be useful, they should be drafted by the church's lawyer.

Because of the particular technicalities associated with the use of liability release forms, it is important for churches that intend to rely upon them to be certain that they are properly drafted. Blanket general waiver forms that are not carefully drafted are likely to have little legal value in many states. They may have some emotional value in that they encourage people not to sue, but blanket general waivers should not be relied upon by churches in limiting their exposure to risk.

In addition to drafting liability waiver forms, churches conducting programs involving minors should be certain that they have properly drafted medical release forms for each of the minors participating in the program (see the sample forms). Without a properly drafted medical release form, the church may find itself in a position in which it is incapable of obtaining medical care for a minor who is injured.

Churches undertaking short-term mission projects to unstable parts of the world may also wish to have a formally drafted policy on how they will handle kidnappings and whether or not they will pay ransom. Participants in the program should be fully aware of the policy and should be required to sign an agreement acknowledging their knowledge and acceptance of the policy. This is particularly true if the church does not intend to pay ransom.[1]

Finally, churches should consider the use of Christian arbitration clauses in their agreements with participants in their programs. The major purpose of these clauses is to shift any dispute over liability from the court system into an arbitration proceeding conducted by other Christians. The primary advantage of this approach is that it gives the church the opportunity to address any dispute in a Christian forum, rather than before a secular jury or judge. It is also often much less expensive to handle disputes through arbitration.

There are potential disadvantages to arbitration as well. Some professionals believe that individuals may be more likely to sue if there is a Christian arbitration clause in the contract. Although this has not been this author's experience, it is a concern for some organizations.

# Liability Release Agreement

The undersigned wishes his or her minor child or ward _____ (herein the "Child") to participate in the following activity: _____ (herein the "Activity") sponsored by the _____, a California nonprofit religious corporation (herein the "Church").

Church and the undersigned agree that the Activity poses risks including the following specific risks: _____

_____

_____, as well as similar and dissimilar risks (herein the "Risks").

For and in consideration of the Church allowing the Child to participate in the Activity, and other good and valuable consideration the receipt and sufficiency of which are hereby acknowledged, the undersigned, for himself or herself, for the Child and the Child's personal representatives, assigns, heirs, distributees, guardians and next of kin (herein the "Releasors"), release, waive, discharge and covenant not to sue the Church and its Board Members, Pastors, officers, employees and agents (herein the "Releasees"), from all liability to the Releasors, on account of injury to the Child or the death of the Child or injury to the property of the Child, whether caused by the negligence of Releasees or otherwise, while the Child is participating in the Activity.

The undersigned is fully aware of the Risks and other hazards inherent in the Activity and is allowing the Child to participate in the Activity, and voluntarily assumes the Risks and all other risks of loss, damage, or injury that may be sustained by the Child while participating in the Activity.

The undersigned warrants that he or she has fully read and understands this Liability Release Agreement and voluntarily signs the same, and that no oral representations, statements or inducements apart from the foregoing written agreement have been made to the undersigned.

Caution: Read Before Signing

_____          _____
Date                  (signed)

_____          _____
(witness)              (please print name)

_____          _____
(please print name)   (relationship to Child)

## Parental Authorization to Consent to Treatment of Minor

_____
Parent or Legal Guardian Herein ("Parent")

_____
(Herein "Minor")

_____
(Herein "Organization")

_____
(Herein "Designated Agent")

The above-named Parent of the Minor has entrusted the Minor into the care of Organization, while the Minor participates in an activity sponsored by the Organization, and for the welfare of the Minor.

The Parent does hereby authorize the Designated Agent of the Organization to consent to any X-ray examination, anesthetic, medical or surgical diagnosis or treatment and hospital care which is deemed advisable by, and is to be rendered under the general or special supervision of, any physician and surgeon licensed under the laws of the State or Country in which the medical care is being sought and on the medical staff of any hospital; or to consent to any X-ray examination, anesthetic, dental or surgical diagnosis or treatment to be rendered to the Minor by any dentist licensed under the laws of the State or Country in which the dental care is being sought.

It is understood that this authorization is given in advance of any X-ray examination, anesthetic, medical or surgical diagnosis or treatment and hospital care being required but is given to provide authority and power on the part of the Designated Agent to give specific consent to any and all such examination, anesthetic, diagnosis, treatment, or hospital care which the aforementioned surgeon, physician and/or dentist, in the exercise of his/her best judgment, may deem advisable.

The Parent hereby authorizes any hospital which has provided treatment to the Minor to surrender physical custody of the Minor to the Designated Agent upon the completion of treatment.

The Parent hereby agrees to fully pay all costs of medical or dental care incurred for the Minor by the Designated Agent under this authorization.

These authorizations shall remain effective until _____ unless sooner revoked in writing delivered to said Designated Agent.

_____   _____
Date        (Parent or Legal Guardian)

# Medical Information

Insurance Company: _____

Claim Office Address: _____

Claim Office Telephone Number: _____

Policy No.: _____

Employer Name and Address: _____

_____

Where Parent Can Be Reached: _____

Telephone: _____

Address: _____

   Special Medical Conditions of Minor, such as Diabetes, Allergic Reactions, Medications Currently Used: _____

_____

_____

Pediatrician:

Name: _____

Address: _____

Telephone: _____

## Resolution of Disputes

The parties to this Contract are Christians and believe that the Bible commands them to make every effort to live at peace and to resolve disputes with each other in private or within the Christian church in conformity with the biblical injunctions of Matthew 5:22–24; Matthew 18:15–20; and 1 Corinthians 6:1–8. Therefore, the parties agree that any controversy or claim arising out of the _____ by _____ which cannot be resolved within _____, shall be resolved with the assistance of the Christian Conciliation Service of _____ County through mediation or, as a last resort, through legally binding arbitration.

The parties agree that these methods shall be the sole remedy for any controversy or claim whatsoever arising out of the _____ by _____ including claims for violations of federal and state law and for negligent or intentional wrongful conduct. The parties further agree that these methods shall be the sole remedy whether the claim is between the _____ and _____ or one or more of its pastors, board members, officers, employees or volunteers. The parties expressly waive their right to file a lawsuit against one another in any civil court for such disputes, except to enforce a legally binding arbitration decision.

SIGNED: _____
DATED: _____

In addition, there is a general belief that arbitrators may be more likely to want to award something in cases where a court might firmly find in favor of the church. There may be some truth to these concerns, but the benefits of being in a Christian forum may well outweigh whatever risk there is of a possible small award. This is particularly true if the issue that gives rise to the dispute has religious overtones.

An example of a Christian arbitration clause is included in this chapter. If this type of clause is going to be used by the church, the participants in the program must sign a contract with the arbitration language in it. It can be incorporated into an overall agreement for the trip or be a separate document. The parents or guardians should sign when minors are participating in the trip.

Several Christian arbitration services are now active throughout the country. The Association of Christian Conciliation Services, founded by the Christian Legal Society, can be contacted at (406) 256–1583.

## Conclusion

Although lawsuits filed against churches are increasing, legal risks are generally quantifiable. Careful planning and good practices can eliminate most of the risks associated with mission projects. Purchasing insurance can fill in the balance of the gap. As a practical matter, even though there has been an increase in the number of lawsuits recently, most of those suits have arisen out of serious intentional wrongs committed by clergy and volunteers on behalf of churches, such as sexual misconduct and invasion of privacy. The courts have not been generally receptive to suits that lack a good legal basis.

In addition, it is crucial that churches operating mission programs give careful thought to the tax and regulatory implications of the programs. The best way to limit exposure to liability in this regard is to obtain the services of a competent attorney to assist with planning and structuring the program.

*Dennis Kasper has been a practicing attorney for the past twenty years. In addition, he serves as a consultant to churches and nonprofit organizations regarding legal matters. He is a member of the board of elders at his home church, First Presbyterian Church of Hollywood, and has written numerous articles integrating law and Christian ministry.*

# 9

# Selecting
# a Sponsoring Agency

## Jack Larson

To go on a mission project is to participate in an assault on enemy territory. This is not a summer camp brought overseas but a spiritual battle with eternal consequences for all involved. Many organizations can assist you in your desire to serve Christ on the foreign field, but I believe the best way to serve is through a local church. The local church is the only institution that has been specifically commissioned by God for the task. However, that is not to say that sponsoring organizations cannot be of significant help. In many cases, the best short-term mission experiences come as a result of a partnership between the local church and a sponsoring organization. The purpose of this chapter is to guide you in selecting a mission organization so you can be sure that the partnership meets your needs as a leader in the local church.

# The Local Church versus a Sponsoring Agency

After over fourteen years of short-term mission group leadership involving taking several thousand participants on projects, I have learned some important lessons. If I could articulate my strongest recommendation for pastors, youth leaders, and church lay leaders it would be this: Do not send people on short-term mission experiences. **Take them!**

The reasons for this statement are many. First, short-term mission experiences can be one of the most challenging events of a person's life. They often have a tremendous impact on the spiritual formation of believers. Because of the impact of the experience, serious life decisions are made. These spiritual milestones are most effective when they are shared by the pastor and the individual.

For example, the training necessary for such a project can be done most effectively by local church leadership. A quality sponsoring organization can assist with materials, guidance, and training, but it should not take over this important dimension of leadership development.

In my early years of leading projects I would advertise, promote, and recruit any individual who could provide me with a pastor's reference, a doctor's permission, and the right amount of money. I soon began to learn the folly of such a practice. I'll never forget Molly, who came by herself with a glowing recommendation from her pastor. From the time she got on the plane with us until the time I gladly waved good-bye to her she was trouble—from verbally assaulting the leadership, to physically assaulting my wife, to sneaking out of camp at night and joining the parties of the nationals. The final straw was broken when at the beach on our off day she went exactly where she wasn't supposed to go, dove in a dangerous area, and dislocated her shoulder. Her injury required surgery and cost us scarce money, loads of staff time, and many frazzled nerves.

Did Molly grow spiritually? It's hard to say, but I doubt it. After listening to and observing her, I'm not sure where she was at spiritually. I do know she was a royal pain to every leader and project participant. When I later called the girl's pastor, the lights began to turn on for me. She rarely attended church, but the girl's mother thought this project might help her wayward daughter. The pastor, at Mom's request, made up a strong recommendation and signed his name. Molly was not a good candidate for an overseas mission experience. She ended up disrupting our entire project and almost ended her life.

I had too many Mollys during my early years before I went against the prevalent philosophy of most of the other organizations at the time, which is "Take who the Lord sends you." I didn't stop to consider that the enemy might also want to send a few of his own to disrupt and derail a mission project meant to strengthen the spiritual maturity of those participating and to challenge them to respond to the needs of the world.

My whole strategy changed to recruiting only church leaders and then helping these leaders recruit, screen, and train their own church volunteers. It is crucial that the church provide leaders who will stay and grow with the participants during the entire experience and then continue the effects back home through follow-up programs. When spiritual gifts of a volunteer are brought to the surface as a result of a short-term project, the pastor is able to help that person channel these gifts into the local church. In addition, the passion for missions that the individuals develop while on the field can be directed toward meeting the mission needs of their own church.

## Criteria for Selecting a Sponsoring Agency

Organizations that are designed to bring volunteers to the mission field for short-term experiences are needed today. However, it is important for church leaders to understand their strengths and weaknesses. The purpose of this section is to give you some practical guidelines as a church leader in selecting a sponsoring organization for a short-term mission experience, particularly if this is your first short-term mission venture.

*Criterion 1:* Choose an organization whose primary reason for being is to serve, assist, and enable the local church to accomplish its mandate and calling. Remember, these agencies are parachurch organizations. By that, I mean that they should recognize the primacy of the local church and seek to assist you in accomplishing your goals and objectives. They are the servant of the church! The mission organization should know that the Great Commission mandate was given to the church. In *The Body,* Chuck Colson states,

> Evangelism should always be designed to bring the convert into the local church, where the work of discipleship can be done. . . . When evangelistic efforts are not integrated with the local church, they run the grave danger of being out of the will of God. For the Great Conversion by definition involves baptism and disciple making and this can only be done in the context of a local confessing congregation.

I don't believe I would be doing a disservice to Mr. Colson by including "missions" in his strong statement. Many Christian organizations by-pass this elementary principle, to the peril of the entire body. Leighton Ford has stated, "Those parachurch Christian organizations that thrive or even survive during this next era will be those organizations that serve and are committed to the local church."

I believe that with all my heart. This may sound ironic coming from one who has served over twenty years with parachurch ministries. But it's true, and every parachurch work needs to occasionally stop and consider its own relationship with the local church and its specialized role of serving, equipping, or assisting the church to do its job well in a specific area of outreach.

If you were to evaluate all organizations offering short-term volunteer involvement (now well over three hundred) based on criterion 1 you would reduce the field dramatically. You might be saying "Hey, wait a minute, that means you've just eliminated many well-known organizations which have been around for a long time." Yes, I have.

You might even have been a participant and grown from the experience. That's great, but that still does not mean that was the best way to have that experience. God will redeem every experience in our life for our growth and his glory. When I was laid up for months with hepatitis in the Dominican Republic I grew tremendously but I would not recommend it to anybody as a means of growth.

*Criterion 2:* Choose an organization that helps you train and equip your volunteers for their short-term experience. Those who direct these mission agencies understand the value of proper training and preparation. They want to be sure that your short-term experience is successful and spiritually beneficial to each member of your group. In order to accomplish this, they should be willing to assist you in this training and equipping.

Keep in mind that the goal of your short-term mission experience is not the project itself. The project that you select to invest in is actually a means to accomplishing your goal. The goal of a short-term missions activity is for the church leader to disciple his or her volunteers. The project may last only a few brief weeks but the relationship that you build with your volunteers will last for years to come.

A quality mission experience needs a full year and a half to complete the cycle (see table 9.1). Notice that training and follow-up make up most of the time. It is unfortunate that many churches and organizations spend the bulk of their time on training and the project itself, with follow-up receiving only minimal priority. Certainly training is an acknowledged goal, but usually the average church is not equipped or experienced in the best training methods and materials. Here is where a quality organization proves its worth.

### Table 9.1
### Timetable for Short-Term Missions Experience

| September: | Select the organization that will lead your group |
| --- | --- |
| October – December: | Promote, recruit, and screen volunteers |
| January – May: | Train and equip the volunteers |
| June or July: | Participate in the short-term experience |
| August – February: | Follow up with each participant |

I can remember so clearly those churches that really used our materials and took training seriously. They saw the project for what it was: not an event but a tool of discipleship. Probably the best tool I've ever seen.

*Criterion 3:* Choose an organization that can most effectively, economically, and safely set up logistics and manage the project.

Churches hire professionals at all levels of church life from custodians to accountants to pastors. They also bring in specialists for brief periods to repair the air conditioning, consult on raising money for the new C.E. wing, or give marriage-strengthening seminars. In the same way, a church leader who is directing a short-term mission experience should hire a consultant or a sponsoring agency that can oversee the myriad of details associated with such an experience.

A quality short-term mission organization frees church leaders to accomplish their specific calling, which is shepherding their group. It is a rare church leader who can do all the logistical set-up, training, and project management. If you include discipleship, counseling, leading morning devotions and evening meetings, follow-up, and other functions of the leader, the project can soon be overwhelming. But that's why many quality organizations have emerged and know that their calling is to enable and encourage church leaders, while the organization provides quality project set-up, training, and operation management.

Some of the logistical areas that a professional sponsoring organization oversees are the following:

*Air travel*—This high-budget item can cause untold waste and headaches if not handled by experienced pros. The best short-term organizations know the most helpful group travel agents. There is no such thing as a "special price" or "special deal." All travel agents have the same prices but do not give the same service, so choose wisely.

*Ground transportation*—This can be a high-budget item in most foreign countries. Some inexperienced sponsoring organizations cut corners by transporting groups in the backs of trucks driven by project leaders from the United States. This means of transportation is to be avoided at all cost. Ensure that you have insured, safe, roomy transport driven by reliable, experienced, licensed national drivers.

*Food*—Most short-term groups can handle some experimentation, but I recommend that you keep it to a minimum. In order to stay healthy and strong, North American volunteers need familiar food and plenty of it. How the food is prepared is crucial, because any lack of hygiene precautions can result in severe sickness.

Regarding water, nothing will put a negative attitude in someone as quickly as drinking bad water. This will result in "turista tummy," "Montezuma's revenge," or other cute names for acute diarrhea. Your sponsoring organization will know where to get filtered or bottled water.

*Project*—For obvious reasons the most qualified group to oversee the project is the sponsoring organization. It will employ a field representative who is in touch with the local needs and resources. It is very difficult for a church leader in North America to micromanage this important element of the mission experience from the church office. Leave this important element to the sponsoring organization to oversee.

*Criterion 4:* Choose an organization that offers the broadest range of service opportunities for your volunteers. Some people have not gone on short-term mission experiences because the trip was perceived as being strictly evangelistic in nature. Such an emphasis scared them away from participating. The gift of evangelism is important, but there are many other gifts such as helps, mercy, encouragement, service, and artistry, all of which are also needed on the mission field. In fact, a mission project is the perfect crucible for discovering and developing these gifts as well.

Select a sponsoring organization that will develop a project that can utilize all of the gifts and abilities that your volunteers bring with them. A good sponsoring organization will take the time to listen to you describe the strengths and weaknesses of your group. From there, they will design and select a project that will maximize the areas of giftedness that your group possesses.

*Criterion 5:* Select a sponsoring organization that is frank with you about expectations, costs, and purpose for involvement. Before you select an organization to partner with, consider the following:

1. Ask for a budget breakdown of the project.
2. Ask for a list of five recent group leaders with phone numbers.
3. Check references to see if reality met advertisements.
4. Ask about affiliations (Evangelical Council for Financial Accountability, National Association of Evangelicals, etc.).
5. Consider which denomination is closest to your theological preferences.
6. Inquire about overseas partnerships with nationally run churches.
7. Consider how the staff makes a living. Who will be going on your project from the organization, and what are their qualifications for leadership?

## Conclusion

Selecting a sponsoring organization is an important step in the process of taking volunteers to the mission field. An organization with experience and a servant attitude can make the difference between a successful trip and one marked by failure. It will cost a few dollars more per volunteer to secure the services of these professionals but when you consider the amount of work they do and the service they provide for you, they are well worth the investment. However, that is not to say that all short-term mission organizations have the same degree of professionalism and concern for church ministry. A great degree of caution must be exercised in the selection of the organization.

In the Mandarin Chinese language, the symbol for crisis is the same as for opportunity. Short-term mission projects that are led by someone unprepared and inexperienced can and usually do create crises. However, a mission project done through a meaningful partnership with an excellent short-term organization produces opportunities for positive spiritual growth.

*Jack Larson has been a short-term missions executive for many years. He founded World Servants, a mission organization dedicated to building up the local church through short-term mission involvement. He is currently serving as a consultant to churches and parachurch organizations across North America in the area of short-term missions.*

# 10

# What I Wish Every Team Knew Before Coming: A Field Representative's Perspective

## *Samuel Melo*

When you go to a different country as a tourist you normally receive some form of orientation. This may come from a book, a travel agent, or perhaps from a guide in the country after you arrive. The local guide is always best because that individual knows the culture, geography, sights, and local habits. Things that visitors may not be taking into account will not be overlooked by the person who actually lives there.

## Advantages of Working with Local Leaders

Each culture that you come into is a new world. To have someone who knows the ins and outs of the country you are visiting can be a tremendous advantage for you. That person can let you know what is appropriate and what is not, and in so doing, can save you a great deal of embarrassment.

Another important advantage to having this local leader is that he or she knows the history of the country and how the gospel came to the people. For example, here in the Dominican Republic, Christopher Columbus and his team of "missionaries" came to the island five hundred years ago on their way to the New World. They came not with a servant attitude but rather with one of superiority and pride. They were the conquering Christians who were sent to "evangelize the natives." They soon lost focus of their mission and became landowners, turning many of the local nationals into indentured slaves. The people they came to reach became their personal property. This resulted in an atmosphere of distrust, and in many cases, open hostility toward anything resembling Christianity. Knowing this historical perspective helps volunteers who come to our island to conduct their ministries.

A third advantage of knowing and using local leaders is that they will have established a network for working with local churches. Having this network is crucial, especially in Third-World and developing countries. In our culture, community living is essential to survive. You cannot try to build a project in a Latin community without networking through the members of the community itself. Those who have tried to establish their own ministry without communicating or networking with the local people are viewed with suspicion and distrust. Obstacles will be put in their way and life can be tedious if not stalled altogether.

A fourth reason for using a local leader to coordinate your project is found in the realities of getting things done in a foreign culture. In most developing countries there is a motto that states, "Never do today what you can put off until next week." Dealings with local government officials move slowly and at their own rambling pace. It appears to the outsider as a bureaucratic entanglement. However, to the local leader who knows how to work within the system, progress can be made and things can get done. Things move only if you know somebody.

For example, if a nonnational leader came to our country and tried to secure a building permit it could take him weeks, perhaps even months. But to the local leader who knows how to work within the system, as unorganized as it may appear to the outsider, a permit can be secured within a few days. If you want to get something done you have to take the time to develop the official's trust and respect. You ask officials about their families, you ask about the welfare of their relatives, you look for ways to establish a relationship first, and only then would you ask for something related to official business. These things must be done *before* the team arrives or the entire project can be stalled.

Lastly, the local leader stays behind and continues the ministry that your group began. When you are the local leader you are not only concerned about the project that you are currently developing but you are also concerned about the future effectiveness of that project. The local leader knows what is truly needed within that community.

One of the problems we face at times is from groups that want to build a new church building. They have in their minds that unless they build a new church, they haven't really done ministry. We have more church buildings in Haiti and the Dominican Republic than we have church members to fill them. Some church buildings have been built but sit empty because the community never wanted a new church building. What they wanted was a center for community health classes. It may not sound as glamorous as a church building but it meets more needs in the local community than another church building. You must take into account what will happen in the community after the group has gone.

## Things to Consider *Before* Arriving on the Field

There are a number of things that a local church leader can do that will help ensure an effective mission experience for the group before it leaves its home church. Groups that give attention to these elements before they come here always have a better and smoother experience.

*Make initial contact with the field representative.* There are various ways to make an initial contact with a field representative in the country you wish to visit. One of the best ways is by word of mouth. Ask around among your pastoral friends and find out who they have used in the past. Getting a personal reference from someone who has already been in the country is a great way to connect with a local ministry leader. Perhaps your church or denomination has a missionary in the country who will have a network of local contacts established already.

Another way is to review literature that is published throughout North America by the many mission agencies that operate overseas. Ask what organizations they work with on the field and who their contact people are.

Once you get the name of a ministry leader on the field, keep in mind that communication with individuals in developing countries can be quite time consuming. If you expect an immediate response from someone who lives in the interior, your expectations may need to be altered. Mail delivery in most developing countries is very slow at best. People you are contacting to determine their willingness to host your group should be contacted by phone when possible. Always be sure to write down your notes and follow up your call with a letter of confirmation. This will eliminate misunderstandings.

*Learn the history of the gospel in the country.* In every country, the nationals have already been targeted by some gospel outreach. In some cases, due to overzealous and insensitive missionaries, this initial contact has left a negative impression on them. Your team's success may be determined by the effects of those individuals who have proceeded you to the country. Remember, in most cases, God has arrived before you, and your involvement is part of an ongoing process of communicating the gospel with the nationals.

For many years I have shared with our visiting teams the importance of trying to avoid the concept I call "I'm bringing God in my pocket," which means that the work of God begins with your arrival and you must do all you can to save as many people as possible during your short missions experience. People get saved the same way in every country—only by his grace and the power of the Holy Spirit—but knowing the history of the gospel in that particular context would help you see the bigger picture and join in partnership with what God is doing and will continue to do in that country.

*Clearly communicate your expectations.* There needs to be a clear understanding of what you want to accomplish as a group. This has been a major area of misunderstanding with groups over the years. It comes to the surface with statements like, "I thought we were going to do more than a construction job," or "I thought you wanted to do this but instead you did that."

When it comes to planning your trip I believe it is important to communicate with the people where you are going what you have in mind that the team would like to accomplish. There are many approaches you can take in serving on a short-term mission experience. If you have in mind to do a building project from beginning to end, then ask how long would it take to accomplish it, what type of materials are necessary, and what amount of funds will be needed. If what you have in mind is to have your team develop friendships, to share their faith without construction projects, then this must be clearly communicated so that the field representative can prepare accordingly. These are all issues that should be discussed sufficiently in advance.

*Establish a foundation of trust between yourself and the field representative.* Trust is the bottom line for a successful project. Trusting takes some degree of courage. You will have to take chances that something may go wrong. This level of trust sets an environment in which communication can be open and expectations can be expressed.

Trusting involves taking a risk with people. This matter of trust also applies when deciding on cultural issues. There are rules that may appear silly to the average North American person, but they may be a key issue in the culture you are visiting. Many of the local Christians in the communities tend to have legalistic views that were taught by missionaries many years ago. The missionaries have caught up with the changes because back where they come from the old-fashioned Christianity (if we may call it that) is no longer taught. The church here still keeps with the legalistic views.

*Ensure adequate orientation before you come.* This usually involves several sessions with your group while you are preparing to come. The content of this training will depend on the nature of your project, but regardless of your intention for coming, some basic understanding of the history, culture, geography, and climate of the country is essential. I suggest you have someone come to your group who has been to the country before and can share from personal experience what it was like. Slides or videos would be helpful as well.

You will need to discuss any significant cultural issues involved in the country you are visiting. For example, if you are going to visit Haiti, you will want to discuss the significant political differences between Haiti and other Caribbean countries. You will also want to explain what voodoo is and how to recognize it. If you visit any remote villages in Haiti, you will surely run into it and will want to be prepared for what you will see.

Several churches that have come to the Dominican Republic in the past have planned a small project for their team to complete while in training to come. This one- or two-day training experience helps build team unity and gets the team into a productive mindset.

*Remember that attitude comes before action.* Your actions will speak louder than what you say by your words. How people will perceive you will often depend upon your attitude and nonverbal communication. You may visit a country where you do not know the language and you might be tempted to think that you are not communicating. This feeling may lead to frustration or even anger with those around you. But the fact is we are always communicating through our expressions, our smiles, our laughs. These nonverbal forms of communication are sending a message about how much you care. It reflects an attitude of your heart.

Jesus taught us to serve the needs of others with an attitude of servanthood. Being a servant is not easy for anyone. I believe it is even harder for someone from North America than it is for a person living in the Third World. If you are not careful, North Americans may come to a Third-World country thinking they are superior because they come from a country with development and know better ways of doing things. In a sense, when you come into a new country you arrive with a different set of glasses, that is, new ways of seeing things from those who live in the host country. You must be willing to lay aside those glasses and say, "I am coming to learn" in addition to having a desire to give.

*Learn a few words of the language before you arrive.* Learning a new language is not easy for most people. You must be willing to take the risk of making a mistake. Sometimes you will use a word that will sound similar to another word. The result may be humiliating. You must be willing to laugh at yourself and move on. Those who take the time to learn a few words in the country they are visiting will communicate respect and appreciation for the nationals. Simple words of greeting, departure, or transportation directions can open up doors of opportunity for you and your team.

No amount of preparation and advance orientation can eliminate all problems or obstacles. Some things are bound to go wrong even after the most detailed plans have been developed. However, the more forethought you give to preparation and training before you depart for your short-term trip, the better off you and your group will be before you arrive.

## Things to Consider *After* You Arrive

There is nothing like the thrill of adventure that fills you the day you arrive in the country for the first time. There is a high level of anticipation and excitement. Your first day is filled with new sights, smells, and strange sounds. If it is the first time you have ever traveled to a Third-World country you will find that things happen differently than in North America. These differences can either be received with a spirit of adventure or become a constant source of frustration and anxiety.

*Expect the unexpected.* Always be prepared for the worst when you are on the mission field. The motto, "If something can go wrong on the mission field, it will go wrong" is not as pessimistic an outlook as you might think. If you have in your mind the idea that "Things can go wrong but that's O.K." then you will be able to enjoy your mission experience regardless of what befalls you.

One way to cope with failed expectations is to readjust them. Have a flexible outlook and make the best out of your new circumstances. For example, you may get a flat tire driving down unmaintained roads in the rural part of the country. In North America you would simply put on a new tire from out of your trunk. Many Third-World cars don't have such luxuries. You will need to walk or hitch a ride with your flat tire to the nearest town and get it fixed—that is assuming the next town up the road has a service station. But what do you do with the team waiting in the van while this repair is taking place? Don't let them sit in the van grumbling and complaining about how "backward and forsaken" this country is. Instead, get them to start playing games with the neighborhood children who by now will have started to gather to stare at the "whites" in their barrio. Sing some songs and tell stories to the children. In essence, start an impromptu Vacation Bible School. See your new change of plans as God's way of taking control over your schedule.

*Have a local leader give your group some orientation once it arrives.* The orientation you received before leaving helped shed some light on the economic conditions of the country. Seeing the sights and experiencing the smells has a way of putting reality into the volunteer's perspective. This leader can explain the history of the country, geographical highlights, current political climate, economic conditions, and religious backgrounds of the people. The leader can answer the questions that are going through the minds of your volunteers and can help explain why things happen the way they do in your particular locale.

One helpful way to conduct this detailed orientation is to go to the highest point of the city, which probably has a monument to a national leader. From this vantage point you can point out the various communities and illustrate how the natural barriers (mountain range, valleys, rivers) have affected the demographic composition of the people.

This orientation should be broad in scope. Explain how North Americans are perceived by the local people. What things would be offensive in this culture and how can the group members be sure they will be accepted by the local people? These are all issues that should be discussed in detail since they will have a profound impact on your ministry.

*Privacy is a foreign concept.* Privacy does not exist in the mind of the average person in a poor community, including your brothers and sisters in Christ. Probably the only place you will experience any degree of privacy is in the bathroom, and in many cultures of South America even that is not a private act. People will want to watch you wherever you go and whatever you do. They are intrigued by your presence in their community and want to know as much about you as they can in the time that you are with them. From their point of view, learning about you involves observing your every action throughout the day *and* night.

Many people in countries like the Dominican Republic have grown up in an environment in which belonging to the group (extended family or community) is a normal part of their upbringing. Individual privacy is discouraged. As your volunteers interact with the community, what may look like total chaos, for the lack of privacy because members of several families are living together, is part of what makes the community function.

There are times when you will want and need privacy as a ministry team. For instance, during a missions experience, as the days pass you will feel the need to be alone or get away as a group to digest the things that are going through your team members' minds. This should be explained to your field representative so any misunderstandings can be avoided. Arrangements can be made for your group to meet in a local school classroom, a church building during the day, or perhaps someone's home for a few hours. Explain to the field representative why you need some time alone and how long you need to meet.

My wife, Sharyn, is from Canada and this has been an adjustment for her. Living in a developing country means there is an abundance of population. Neighborhoods are crowded, streets are congested, and everywhere you go you will find many people there before you. Sharyn has had to learn that people will always be in our home. There is a constant flow of family and friends in our home. That is our culture and the way we live. It involves a sensitivity to the culture so as to not give an offense to someone.

*Balance between project and people is necessary.* In my view, a project for any team should include a combination of relational ministry and physical labor that is done as an expression of love. Coming to serve in a poor nation with the team prepared to do a series of evangelistic meetings in the streets, local churches, or hospital can be very rewarding, since the people need hope and are very open to the gospel. Relational ministry is warmly received by the people in the villages.

But in addition to this kind of ministry, the people also need material resources. They need schools, community health clinics or hospitals, vocational training centers. The government has not given them a listening ear. Something as practical as a well for water can make such a difference to a community. Projects, in a real sense, can unlock the door of ministry opportunity to people in a local village. As they participate with you in building a needed community resource, they will be more receptive to hearing the message as to why you have come. Refer to chapter 4 for a more detailed discussion on this topic. For now, let me say that a balance of both is needed when you come.

*Health and safety issues.* Of prime importance is the observation of hygiene in food preparation. Be very careful about the water. A small amount of bad water can have a profound effect on the ministry effectiveness of your group. Not following even small instructions can devastate your group's health. Try and find a balance here too. You don't want to be so paranoid to the extent that you neglect to experience and enjoy the local foods. However, sometimes only the locals can tolerate the kinds of foods that they prepare and eat. This is an area in which you must trust and respect the advice of the field representative without hesitation.

In almost all cases, your group should not consume food that is prepared on the street. Local vendors do not maintain a high standard of health and hygiene. Most of their customers have conditioned stomachs and are not affected by small amounts of amebas or parasites in the food. North American stomachs, on the other hand, are extremely fragile. Don't let anyone in the group show off by eating local foods from street vendors. The issue is not the consumption of the food but rather what happens hours, or perhaps days and weeks, later. Some microscopic organisms, especially in South American and central Asian countries, can remain in the human intestinal tract for the rest of one's life.

If volunteers in your group require specialized medications, tell them to bring enough for the entire time, and even a little extra in case their travel plans change. Many foreign clinics will not have the more advanced medicines that are commonly available in North America. Know the medical history of each of your volunteers. Keep documents such as medical histories and liability release forms with you whenever you travel. Know who in your group has what blood type and who might be prone to heat stroke or asthma.

Be sure you explain to the team members that it is essential for them to follow the directions of the field representative. They may not always understand why the directions are being given, but it must be assumed at all times that they are for the members' own good.

*Handling finances in the host country.* Dealing with finances has the potential for being a headache for you if you have not clearly communicated expectations and costs. Having a clear understanding about what the finances will cover before you arrive will help alleviate misunderstandings after you arrive. Whenever possible, refer to a written budget that both the field representative and the group leader have agreed upon prior to arrival.

The group leader needs to understand that certain costs will be incurred before the group arrives. Advance deposits are essential for the field representative to purchase food, building supplies, or transportation. Many of these expenses will have to be paid for even before the group arrives, so giving a financial advance is usually required.

I have had groups who felt disappointed because their building was not finished or their project was not complete before they left for home. Perhaps the building supplies were not purchased or delivered on time or the group ran out of money. In some cases the disappointment could have been prevented if better communication had taken place regarding their finances.

In some situations finances have been used as a way to manipulate events. Some pastors feel that because they have the money they can control how it is used. Things work differently in foreign cultures. In some cases, you will have to pay for things in advance and trust that the individual will deliver the materials you ordered on time. When North American pastors come and forcefully try to change how purchases are made and how materials are delivered, they may find themselves with no supplies for the project they want to build. Local villages may want the project and may want the business you bring, but they are not willing to sacrifice their pride and self-respect to get it. Let the field representative purchase the materials and arrange for delivery.

Don't always expect to get a formal cash register receipt for all of your purchases. Many village shops are simply not run that way. The shop owner's cash register is his coat pocket! Many have learned to run successful family-owned businesses for many years without learning how to read or write. They couldn't write a receipt if you asked. In addition, our culture dictates a high level of trust among our members. If people say they will do something for you, they will do it. You would never ask them to prove it by putting their statements in writing. The same is true for business deals. Asking for a receipt would be a sign of distrust. If your church accountant back home needs a record of expenses, bring along a notebook and a supply of petty-cash vouchers. Keep a record as you go along and have your field representative or a team member verify financial disbursements.

One last area of importance in this regard is how you handle your finances before people, especially in poor communities where you may be working. You will probably be confronted with a lot of needs and you might feel overwhelmed. As you walk through the village you may be tempted to help by pulling out a dollar bill every time you see someone in need. As much as that might be helpful to some individuals for a brief moment, for the long run it will be detrimental to the ministry. You will be gone in a few days, but your local field representative will have to turn people away for days and months to come. As heartbreaking as it may be at the time, giving money to beg-gars on the street is not a good idea. Put money into the economy by supporting the shops. It builds the self-respect of those who have earned it and reinforces biblical teachings of stewardship. If you want to support those who are poor and cannot work in the commu-nity, give your money to the field representative, missionary, or a local pastor who can see that it goes to those who are truly in need and in a just distribution.

## Conclusion

God has brought hundreds of groups to the Dominican Republic over the many years that I have been here. In that time I have seen remarkable changes take place in the lives of volunteers and group leaders. These groups have also had a profound effect upon the lives of the poor and needy in our communities. It has been one of my greatest joys in life to be a part of the mission experiences of so many people. My family and I have developed friendships with individuals which will last for decades to come.

I have seen just about every possible scenario during these years. As I look back I must say that the groups that got the most out of their mission experience were the ones who came prepared and clearly communicated their expectations. It was my joy to help make their dreams come true. The team that is well oriented and trained before it arrives makes the smoothest transition into a new culture. In addi-tion, it gets the most out of the experience and leaves feeling fulfilled and wanted.

Clear and open communication between the group leader and the field representative is the essential key to the success of the group. Never forget that things happen differently in a Third-World country than they do in North America. If you can keep a sense of humor and realize that God is still in control of the events which to you at times may seem to be so out of control, then you and your group will not just survive the mission experience but truly enjoy your days, and your adventure will be a wise investment in the life of your church.

*Samuel Melo is the executive director of Youth for Christ in the Domin-ican Republic. In this capacity he has directed hundreds of short-term mis-sions trips for North American churches and organizations.*

# 11

# Training and Preparing for the Trip

## Carolyn Koons

When an athlete competes in the Olympic Games it is often just a few brief moments of competition. A short descent from a diving board to the water below or a brief routine on a piece of equipment and the moment in the spotlight is over. What many people don't stop to consider is the vast amount of energy spent preparing for the event itself. Spectators don't see the months and years spent in early-morning practice or late-night discipline. Why does it take so much training to compete? Because to be the best requires nothing less.

In the same way, to be successful in a ministry endeavor requires prayer, preparation, and training. Why should we give Christ any less than our best when we serve him? This chapter is designed to help the church leader understand what should be included in preparing volunteers to participate on a short-term missions trip. We'll examine who should do the training and the timetable that such preparation usually requires. I'll also include a sample six-week training course that we use when we train groups for short-term trips.

## The Director of Leadership Training

At the Institute for Outreach Ministries we help train and prepare over five thousand mission volunteers each year. We take our job seriously because we know how critical training is to the success of the trip as a whole. That's why we work with the youth pastor, singles pastor, associate pastor, or whoever is in charge of the group to be sure that the volunteers are ready when they arrive on the field.

The best person to be responsible for training volunteers for mission service is the pastor of the local church. It is the pastor who knows the unique needs of his or her congregation. This person knows the background of each person attending the trip and how best to modify the training materials to attain maximum effectiveness.

The job of the sponsoring agency is to provide the pastor with all of the necessary materials so that the pastor can be effective in the training phase of the trip. We send each group leader a packet of materials that includes essential training information. We make personal contact and keep in touch throughout the year with each church. We don't wait until the group arrives on the field to begin training. That approach to ministry preparation is shortsighted. Our philosophy of training includes the leadership of the local church. Our job is to ensure the success of these leaders.

## The Purpose of Short-Term Missions Training

There are several reasons why an individual needs to be prepared to serve on the mission field. The first reason is to begin building a group of individuals into a team of volunteers with a common vision. Anyone can assemble a group of people together, but it takes a leader to be able to take them and mold them into a team. Each individual joins the mission team with his or her own motives and goals. As they progress through the training phase of the experience, they should begin to take on the group's motives for service and the group's goals to accomplish.

Chris Eaton and Kim Hurst, in *Vacation with a Purpose* (pp. 92–93), form an acronym to illustrate the importance of teamwork on the short-term mission team. It goes like this:

T is for Teachable
> A teachable spirit helps create a noncompetitive environment in which learning and sharing come naturally. Teachability gives all members the freedom to make mistakes as they learn.

E is for Encouraging
> Think of how encouraging words enhance the development of a community. What differences do they make?

A is for Appreciative
> What things can we appreciate in others on the team? How can we show our appreciation?

M is for Motivated
> Take initiative! Do all things as unto the Lord! (Col. 3:17, 23).

W is for Willing
> Team members may have different levels of strength, skill, and health, but each should be willing to work to the best of his or her capabilities. Willingness also includes accepting uncomfortable conditions in the host country. Willingly take on the heat, food, bugs, and germs.

O is for Open
> Be open with what you are learning, experiencing, feeling, thinking. Express both the positive and negative. Your vulnerability with others builds community.

R is for Refreshing
> The times may be tough—heat, sickness, exhaustion, physical labor, emotional drain, and so on. In those times it will be incredibly refreshing to have another team member help pick up your spirits! Think about how you can be replenishers to each other on a daily basis.

K is for Kindred Spirit
> There's a sense of camaraderie as we pursue this together. We are all part of the Christian family and we're all in this together!

F is for Flexible
> Anything can change from day to day. A flexible team member will learn to accept the unexpected as the norm.

A is for Agreeable
> Living together in close quarters, sharing crowded bathing facilities, and every other aspect of group travel requires everyone to be gracious.

C is for Cooperative
> Share with one another, help and assist one another. Instead of grumbling about problems, propose solutions!

T is for Thoughtful
> What can you do to make a teammate's day a little easier?

O is for Obedient
> There will be times when the team leader has to "pull rank" and make unpopular decisions. A team player will respect the leader's authority and encourage others to do the same.

R is for Relational
> Get to know the others on your team. Go out of your way to learn about their hopes, their dreams, their history.

> Get the picture! The TEAMWORK FACTOR spells out the difference between a group of isolated individuals and a team of interconnected members.

The second purpose for training is to enable the volunteers to open their hearts to the culture and the people of the host country. This does not come naturally to people because we all have our own personal biases and preferences. An effective minister is able to overlook personal preferences (prejudices) in order to serve the needs of others. As the apostle Paul said, "Your attitude should be the same as that of Christ Jesus: Who, being in very nature God, did not consider equality with God something to be grasped, but made himself nothing, taking the very nature of a servant, being made in human likeness" (Phil. 2:5–7 NIV). Being open to other cultures with an open heart is essential for effective service.

The third purpose for training is to develop experience. You want to be sure that the volunteers will be trained in the areas in which they will serve. These areas may include things like leading singing, directing games, teaching a Bible story, making a children's craft, sharing a testimony, or acting in a dramatic performance. This period of practice and honing of skills can make a big difference in building confidence and refining effectiveness.

The fourth purpose is to provide an arena in which volunteers can worship Jesus Christ. After all, service should flow out of an attitude of worship. Time spent as a group in singing and other forms of worship can have a dramatic effect on the formation of spiritual values and attitudes.

The fifth purpose is to discuss information concerning the mission trip. It is important that the volunteers know the specifics about the trip so as to dispel any unrealistic expectations. Questions should be answered, anxieties addressed, and logistics discussed.

The final purpose is to foster an attitude of understanding, service, and learning toward other cultures. For many of the people who volunteer to go on a missions trip this will be their first exposure to another culture. Some time is needed to prepare these individuals for the things they will encounter.

# Pre-Field Training Sessions

There are a variety of ways in which team training sessions can be done effectively. Each leader has an individual style and way of leading. We have many teams going out each year and every team is very different. We suggest you be aware of your own strengths and ask those around you who have experience to help when appropriate. We have provided a general outline of concepts that can be included in training as well as an actual six-week training schedule from one of our previous short-term trips. These general sessions can be adapted according to the availability of experts in the field, team meeting schedules, and length of training.

### Session 1

The primary focus of this session is to allow the team to get to know each other and to go over logistics such as passports or support letters. This meeting is key in setting the tone of the team. For example, what elements do you want students to take home with them concerning the attitudes and climate of the team (praise, worship, fun, relaxing, or whatever is important to you as a leader)?

### Session 2

The focus of this session is to create an environment in which team bonding can take place. There are many ways to communicate what being a team member is all about. There may be a team bonding game that integrates working together on a project and having to focus on what part of the group each individual plays. These can offer great discussion around the roles in the group and how everyone contributes to make a team.

Another option would be to use a learning-style inventory, such as Kolb's, to discuss the different ways people learn and how we can support one another in our strengths and weaknesses. This creates an open environment where people are allowed to discuss who they are and how they fit into a team.

## Session 3

The focus of this session is on culture. A discussion or presentation may be given of the host culture by a person from that country (if possible). This might be done by attending an ethnic church in your area and having a meal at an ethnic restaurant or one prepared by church members. Following this would be a discussion/debrief of stereotypes, differences, and values—both intrinsic and extrinsic—of the host culture and our culture, and anything else the team thinks is important from the experience. It should be clear to the team that they are the learners and the people of the church are the teachers.

If this type of field experience is not possible, many simulation games can create a similar experience that can be debriefed the same way (Intercultural Press has many simulation games).

## Sessions 4, 5, and 6

These sessions depend on the nature and primary ministry of the mission team. They can be used for drama training, VBS preparation, sports, or medical training/practice.

It is also important to spend quality time devoted to preparing testimonies (three minutes or so), developing sermons if appropriate, and learning key tools of evangelism during these training times.

All training sessions could include the following: language acquisition, devotions, sharing, worship in the language to practice and in English to praise, discussion of important logistics, and information concerning how the trip is progressing.

We take our team members on a short field trip to Ensanada, Mexico, to culminate our training program. This is an invaluable time that allows the team to work and learn together in an environment in which team unity, ambiguity, and openness to others' ideas are stressed. The quality of learning that happens on this short experience is invaluable. We use a weekend or a week-long trip depending on the length of the mission experience and the amount of previous training. If it is not possible for any training to occur prior to the trip then a five-day or longer pre-trip is suggested.

What follows is a sample of our training program for students who are participating on a short-term missions experience during the summer. It involves six meetings altogether.

## SHORT-TERM MISSION EXPERIENCE
### Destination: Dominican Republic

### TEAM MEETING 1

This session is the day after the acceptance letters go out. This can be a pizza dinner or dessert time during which team members can get to know each other. *It is important to have this team meeting as soon as you can after the team members receive their acceptance letters.*

STEPS TO COVER:
1. Welcome and prayer
2. Introductions
     Team members introduce themselves and tell why they want to go. If time allows this could be done in pairs and team members could introduce each other. Or you may have a team building game you want to play. Whatever you choose to do, make it enjoyable.
3. Logistics
     Give an overview/timeline as you go over the following sections:
   • Support letter (assign them to be done in a week)
   • Double Your Dollars brochure
   • Discuss financial obligations
   • Passport information
   • Explain Barnabas Prayer Supporters
   • Give out Barnabas Prayer Cards

4. Fundraisers
   Give an overview on fundraising. Discuss ideas for fund-raisers.
5. Special needs
   Share with the team some of the areas in which extra help or research is needed. Ask for volunteers to talk to a leader after the meeting.
6. Announce date and time of next meeting.
7. Close with team prayer time.

ASSIGNMENTS (due the following week)
1. Have a draft of the prayer letter
2. Work on Barnabas Prayer Cards
3. Work on passport

## TEAM MEETING 2

STEPS TO COVER:
1. Welcome and prayer
2. Follow up on Session 1
   - Support letters
   - Passports
   - Barnabas Prayer Cards
   - Fundraiser
   a. Decide on a fundraiser
   b. Divide tasks and responsibilities
   - Make pre-trip assignments
   - Transportation needs
   - Food preparation
   - Worship leaders
   - Photography
   - Equipment
3. Logistics
   - Discuss specific items and preparation needed for project such as construction, medical, sports, children's ministry
   - Go over calendar dates
   - Check parents' addresses
   - Go over shots needed
   - Go over any field trips scheduled
     Example: Child Evangelism Training

- Give out prayer request forms to fill out
- Announce times for team picture to be taken
4. Prayer partners

     Give each team member a 3x3 index card. Ask members to write out their personal prayer request on it to go on the back of their Polaroid photo. Get volunteers to take the Polaroids and tape the requests on them. Pair up and send out. Encourage team members to meet with their prayer partners to pray together.
5. Team prayer time
6. Language learning

     Invite someone to help you learn your names in the language of the country you are going to. Teach a simple Christian song.

ASSIGNMENTS
  1. Mail support letters to potential supporters.
  2. This week's prayer topic is team unity or personal preparation.

## TEAM MEETING 3

1. Take the team picture
2. Prayer
3. Team update sheet

     Pass around the update sheet so students can check off the areas they have completed. For example: prayer letter, passport, Barnabas Prayer Card
4. Team responsibilities

     Continue to share areas of responsibilities in which volunteers are needed. For example: recreation equipment coordinator, special music and drama group for worship services
6. Team initiative exercise
7. Team prayer time

     Option for Session 3: Continue with language learning

ASSIGNMENT
  1. Week's prayer topic is team unity or personal preparation.

TEAM MEETING 4

1. Welcome and prayer
2. Special music and drama
   - Anyone want to do solos, duets?
   - Drama people need to get together and decide what to use
3. Fundraiser
   - Report from a team member on what is doing in his or her life in this area
4. Other finance concerns
   - Two-hundred-dollar deposit due by _____
   - All prayer letters should be out by now
   - How many going to home churches over Thanksgiving/ Christmas?
   - Meet with pastor
   - Speak at youth groups and Sunday school classes
   - Talk with people (that you sent letters to, etc.)
5. Language familiarization and Spanish songs
   A student who speaks Spanish fluently is invited to work with us on Spanish phrases and songs.
6. English songs
7. Devotional
8. Prayer

ASSIGNMENT
1. Weekly prayer topic is the host community.

TEAM MEETING 5

1. Welcome and prayer
2. Cross-cultural awareness
   We invited a guest speaker who knew the Dominican Republic well to join us. She shared about the culture in the Dominican Republic and Catholicism. Examine your stereotypes. Learn to be a bridge builder.
3. Review logistics on Child Evangelism Training Saturday morning
   - Who will drive?
   - VBS coordinators share
4. Go over pre-trip packing

5. Information packet

Give these out to the team and go over each sheet with students. Explain each form; have students fill them out and return them to you. When you have gotten these forms back from the students, return this information so it can be kept with the student's file.

The packets consist of the following:
- "Release of liability"
- "Authorization to treatment"
- "Medical emergency info"
- "Arrival info"
- "Holiday or summer address"

7. Song sheets and tape
8. General announcements
- More prayer cards
- Prayer brochures
- Volunteers for travel alarms
- Extra piece of luggage for sports, VBS, hospitality, etc.
- Hospitality gifts (change from four to two since not in homes)
- Need to see: rec. people, food people, equipment
- Sermons

ASSIGNMENTS
1. Continue to practice song sheet and tape.
2. Weekly prayer topic is either the missionaries the team will work with or the sending church.

### TEAM MEETING 6

1. Meet in the school office at 8:00 A.M.
- Donuts and orange juice
- Pray together before going
2. Child Evangelism Training at Bellflower, California
- Wordless book
- How to teach a Bible verse
- Spanish songs
3. Devotions
4. Back at school office by 1:00 P.M.

ASSIGNMENT
  1. Team work day on children's ministry.
  2. Weekly prayer topic is children's ministry while in the DR.

# Conclusion

The purpose of this chapter has been to reflect a little on why training volunteers is so essential to short-term missions. A number of purposes were discussed. Perhaps you could add a few yourself. In addition to these purposes I have given an overview of what should be included in a short-term training program. Obviously you will need to modify the content to fit your specific destination and team goals.

As the leader of the group you should view your responsibilities beyond those of simply preparing the group to minister on a short-term experience. See your role as a discipler and molder of spiritual formation and this training program as one component of many to help you prepare and train leaders for life-long service to the King of kings!

*Carolyn Koons is the executive director of the Institute for Outreach Ministries at Azusa Pacific University. She has authored and coauthored several books and is a popular conference speaker. She has appeared on numerous radio and television programs.*

# Part 3

# Mission Projects Close to Home

Somehow mission projects accomplished far away are viewed with more glamor and excitement than local missions. What we forget is that the Great Commission requires us to be involved in local missions as a basis for and priority of foreign missions. The church that neglects local missions strictly for the support of foreign missions is misled. Both are essential for a balanced church missions program.

The following section is written by individuals with a passion for local missions involvement. These church mission leaders have experienced the excitement of watching their volunteers catch the vision of local missions. They write with an enthusiasm based upon experience.

The first step in the process is discovering and expanding a church's commitment to local mission opportunities. Ministry in downtown urban settings is a growing area of mission involvement as more and more people move into the inner city. There is much a church can do to minister in this setting if it takes the time to listen to the ministry experts in this section. The final chapter on conducting a world hunger day at your church is practical and guaranteed to work.

# 12

# Discovering and Expanding Local Outreach Activities

## *Karen Taulien*

Most of us who have grown up in the church can remember being awestruck by the stories that were told by missionaries who had just returned from the jungles of South America or remote parts of Africa. We listened with amazement as the missionaries described the challenges they faced while living in such primitive settings. There was a certain appeal about serving the Lord in such challenging locations, as if the more remote you went with the gospel, the more spiritual you were. Although such an attitude has no scriptural basis, it is still quite prominent among believers today. To some, the thought of traveling overseas seems to be more appealing than crossing the street. The result is a loss of enthusiasm for local outreach programs of the church.

This attitude was one of the challenges that I encountered when I served as the director of Mariners Local Outreach, or MLO as it is called at our church. MLO is the home missions program of our church. It has grown to such overwhelming proportions over the past few years that the stories told by members of our congregation involved in weekly MLO activities have dwarfed those told by missionaries returning from the foreign field. In essence, local outreach has become a significant foundation at our church.

But how did such a program come into being and how can you ignite your congregation into serving enthusiastically in local mission activities? The answers to these questions may not be as easy to explain. Nevertheless, these are the questions I will seek to answer in this chapter.

## How Bright Is Your Light?

Much of this chapter is about helping people understand what it means to be one of the many unique and precious lights that shine in the darkness as part of the city on the hill. As professional church leaders, I believe our job is to gather these lights—people—and then plug them into service—ministry. We are called to create a one-of-a-kind city-on-a-hill light show that is glorifying to God. Jesus put it this way:

> You are the light of the world. A city on a hill cannot be hidden. Neither do people light a lamp and put it under a bowl. Instead they put it into its stand, and it gives light to everyone in the house. In the same way, let your light so shine before men, that they may see your good deeds and praise your Father in heaven. [Matt. 5:14–16]

A great example of this comes from a television show called *Northern Exposure*. There is a DJ whose weekly task is to bring the people of Cicely, Alaska, some new spiritual perspective. In this particular episode he becomes obsessed with gathering light bulbs from everyone. The interesting part is that he doesn't let people give him just any light bulb. He focuses on the bulbs that only they can offer him—"that black light you had three years ago" or "the one you had in the corner by the couch." In the end he calls the town together at night for his unveiling. They all wait outside in the dark and cold wondering what in the world he could do with all those light bulbs. Then, in a blinding moment, a wall of light is created and he begins to read Scriptures about light. The lesson? The people could look at *their* bulb and see that not only were they necessary to complete the larger light, but also unique within it.

Our churches are filled with people who don't realize how unique their light is or how important it is to the total light show of their church. If you had asked me a number of years ago what I felt my light looked like, I couldn't have answered you with any degree of certainty. But now, after years of involvement in local mission activities, I know what my light looks like and I am learning how to make it brighter and more effective within our corporate light show at Mariners church. My prayer is that you will find something in these pages that will become the inspiration for gathering the lights within your church that together will break forth like the dawn.

## Some Things Aren't Negotiable

There are hundreds of books available for you to learn about the poor and needy, but to begin a ministry only one book is absolutely necessary—the Bible. If you do not have a biblical philosophy of ministry you will have no ministry at all in the long run.

I would encourage you to get a team together and to study at length what God has to say about the poor and needy among us. We have developed a manual that includes study from five major areas of the Bible that speak to a believer's responsibility in helping the poor and needy:

1. Pentateuch: Genesis–Deuteronomy
2. Wisdom Literature: Proverbs–Song of Solomon
3. Prophets: Isaiah–Malachi
4. Gospels: Matthew–Luke
5. Paul's Epistles: Romans–Titus

Time and space do not allow a detailed exposition of each section but let me illustrate what we discovered from the Gospels. I hope it will motivate you to take the time to gather a group of mission leaders together and discuss the findings of each section.

The poor are frequent subjects of Jesus' parables. In Luke 14:1–14 he gives a clue as to why his ministry among the poor received such attention. He is at a meal with an apparently wealthy Pharisee, observing the guests jockey for positions of honor closest to the head of the table. His message to the guests is that "everyone who exalts himself will be humbled and he who humbles himself will be exalted" (v. 11). Then he turns to the host with a message on how to genuinely host a dinner party. He instructs him not to invite his rich friends or anyone with the capacity to pay him back. Rather, he is to invite the poor because they do not have the means to do anything in return. That is what makes a man blessed.

That message to the host contains the reasons why Jesus put such a premium on our ministry among the poor. We minister to those who have no capacity to repay us because such action is a reflection of God's ministry to us. Just as the poor have little, if anything, to give back to us when we minister to them, we also have nothing to give back to God when he takes the initiative with us. Our ministry among the poor is a lesson to us of God's unconditional love.

One of our volunteer team members was so struck by this realization that she wrote in her report, "I was surprised by the evidence . . . I was 'startled awake' by the responsibility I have to be concerned for the poor. Far from a passing concern, I have a responsibility before God—a responsibility which, through his spirit, I hope to fulfill."

## Getting Organized for Local Mission Action

Once you have concluded the study of God's heart for the poor the real fun begins! You now have a group of ten or so people who are committed to changing not only your church, but also the community. You will soon realize an organizational chart is going to have to be a part of this ministry. Someone is going to have to be chairman. What are the tasks of a chairman? What will you do? How does the church fit in? How do ministries fit in? Who are the ministries we should support and/or become involved with? The list is endless. Again, I encourage you to get a team together to sort it out. Over the past six years we have gone through several variations on a theme with our organizational structure. Figure 12.1 will give you a look at what it includes today.

All of the positions are filled by volunteers with the exception of the staff administrator (myself), who is designated half time to MLO. Each position has a detailed and measurable job description. Briefly the roles are these:

**Figure 12.1**

## Mariners Church Local Outreach Organizational Chart

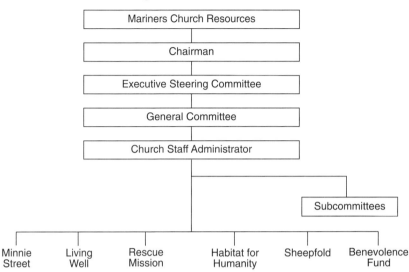

*Mariners Church Resources.* This includes people and money. Its what we have to work with. Its complete strength and capacity is unknown, but thought to be exceptional!

*Chairman.* This is the person who "drives" the ministry and works closely with the staff administrator to keep the ball rolling.

*Executive Committee.* Made up of six to eight people who protect, teach, and develop the mission and vision of MLO. They help with financial planning; educate the body at large on God's heart for the poor; plan, facilitate, dream, hold the rest of MLO and the church accountable.

*General Committee.* Made up of nine to twelve subcommittee members and liaisons who are implementors of vision—doers.

*Staff Administrator.* Coordinates all aspects of MLO—committees, ministries, church at large.

*Liaisons.* Each ministry MLO supports has an identified liaison person to serve as the primary connector between our steering committee and their particular ministry.

The Executive Committee plays a strong leadership role in the program. The members contribute their goals and dreams and help shape the direction of the overall program. They gather together for a half-day twice a year to review the accomplishment of previous organizational goals and for planning future endeavors. I would encourage you to begin with an Executive Steering Committee to establish the following for your ministry.

| | |
|---|---|
| Mission Statement | A broad sentence describing why you exist |
| Vision Statement | Your mission in measurable terms |
| Values/Distinctives | What you hold to be most important as you accomplish your mission |
| Goals | Measurable benchmarks to hold you accountable |
| Resources | Where and how you will get your financial support as well as time from volunteers |
| Relationship to other church agencies | How you relate to foreign missions, the choir, small groups, etc. At Mariners, local outreach (home missions) and global impact (foreign missions) are separate entities. |

How often should the group meet and why?

How do we communicate to the church at large?

How do we educate the church at large?

There is nothing more exciting than seeing a group of volunteers become a cohesive ministry team as they wrestle through this step in organizing a ministry. It doesn't need to happen in one sitting. The time invested in these exercises will pay dividends beyond belief in ownership and loyalty to a young ministry.

## Hitting the Streets

Once you have gone through the process listed you are ready for the most exciting step of all. Finding out who the people in your community are that God has called you to serve. Be careful. This will be the first test for your group as you must put into practice all the study and mission statements you have developed.

Our ministry has developed four criteria for support that have remained constant over the years. It hasn't always been easy to find

**Figure 12.2**
**Determining a Constituency**

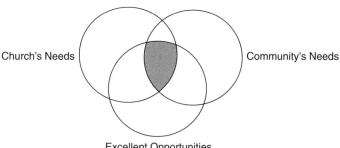

ministries that fit but since we are committed to the biblical basis for our local outreach program, we have not altered the criteria.

1.  The organization is committed to openly proclaiming the gospel.
2.  The organization is to have direct discipleship contact with the people to whom they minister.
3.  The organization provides opportunities for ongoing involvement by members of our church.
4.  The organization is able to demonstrate responsible stewardship in meeting its stated objectives and in handling funds.

Another trap in choosing ministries is trying to meet the needs of a broad range of constituencies. Figure 12.2 helps illustrate the various entities that compete for attention. You will need to walk a delicate line between accommodating each of these important audiences.

Another important consideration here is the need to find a balance between developing spectators and developing participants. For a variety of honest reasons many people cannot get involved in serving in local outreach projects. They may pray, give financially, or encourage others to get involved. On the other hand, many members can and should get involved in local outreach projects. What is needed is finding the balance between the two.

The socioeconomic composition of our church is such that it is easy for folks to write sizeable checks to meet worthy needs. When we first began MLO we simply asked our church members to give money. However, in time we soon discovered a better way. Instead of making an appeal for money, we now distribute a list of items that are needed by the various organizations we support. We ask our people to go to the store as a family and purchase these items themselves and bring them to the church. That way they have a chance to get personally involved in serving the needs of the poor and to teach valuable lessons to their children at the same time.

Another consideration is the importance of seeking a broad range of organizations to support. We are currently involved with two women's and children's shelters, one men's mission, two ministries that focus on children, two convalescence homes, one group that builds affordable housing, and one medical clinic that helps women with unplanned pregnancies. In the next year we would like to add three to four ministries ranging from prison ministry to AIDS ministry. We also have a benevolence fund for people within our own church. This ministry is changing because the church has added a recovery ministry. Up until now we have met only financial needs within a clearly defined policy. Our benevolence fund policies can be found at the end of the chapter for your review. We look forward to being able to help those among us in a way that will meet not only physical but emotional needs.

## Building Relationships Is Critical to Long-Term Success

Many of us in professional church ministry have seen flash-in-the-pan ministries. In local outreach ministries the key to long-term success is building relationships. You may have the best biblical foundation and a well-designed organizational chart, but if you don't have relationships with the people in your church and within the ministries you have chosen, your ministry to the poor and needy in your community will not stand the test of time.

Over the years that I have been directing MLO I have found that those who get involved beyond a casual level are those who have established relationships with others in their ministry. They brought a friend with them the first time they came, or they have bonded with someone in the ministry area. The best way is to start with your leadership team and have them get their friends involved. Then, together, make friends with those who volunteer. You'll soon learn the lesson that people who work together for a common cause have the strongest bond. There are two ways to build these types of relationships: work and play.

*Work.* Convince your ministries to let you work for them—landscaping, painting, tearing walls down, building houses. It helps to build on your foundation of ministry. It also builds excitement because each person will go home and talk about what he or she did, or met some great new people and helped to make a difference.

I have come back from work days that included a CPA, a family counselor, a general contractor, a real estate developer, a mortgage banker, and few college students and have really been able to say they were my friends. Most of the time we are tired, sore, and dirty. But we are always all smiles and ready to go again. These are people I would never have been involved with except for local outreach.

*Play.* We have developed several special events that include people from the ministries we support or just raise funds for them. One is a day for the kids we call "Concrete Cowboy." People from Mariners pick up kids from ministries in Los Angeles and Orange counties and take them to a park where there is a lake, horses, a baseball field. By the end of the day many kids want to go home with the people from church and the feeling is mutual. These relationships keep people involved in trying to make a difference.

Another is our annual Spring Cleaning/Auction/Talent Show. It is a mouthful, but it works. We have people bring their stuff for sale or auction. We eat a BBQ dinner together. Then we see people we love, and used to respect, share their better-left-unknown talents with us. It is an all-church event that gives people several opportunities to become involved with local outreach and meet new friends.

Building this sense of community is one part of this ministry that is the hardest to accomplish and most difficult to measure. People have so many reasons why they can't get involved "at this time." However, I guarantee you the cost of this book, that if you can get them to become friends with the people they are working with or serving, you will never get them to leave your ministry.

## Measuring Your Fruit

It is easy in ministry to decide before a project or event what you think the fruit of it should be. For example: You decide to go to Los Angeles and demolish several walls in a building that is going to become a work center for a ministry. Your goal is to get all the walls down and cleared out by the end of the day. For a lot of reasons, only six of the fifteen volunteers who said they would show up actually appear and all of the girls come with a friend. You finally get to L.A. and discover there are no tools to use even though the leaders of the organization said everything you needed would be there. Luckily, one of your guys is a general contractor who planned ahead and can at least get the group going. It would seem this day is a disaster. It isn't. A banker had a past as a construction worker. Women can hit walls harder than you think: something about working smarter not harder! And making piles of garbage is easy for everyone. We all came back with a very real picture of what the riots had done, how difficult life is in Los Angeles, and new friends.

My point is simply that the shiny red apple is not the only fruit an apple tree bears that is of value. Some apples fall to the ground and may appear dirty and useless, but if you look carefully they are really great to eat. Some are better for pie, but still have value. Please don't get caught in the trap of measuring God's work in this type of ministry by man's ruler. Some specific types of fruit follow:

*Giving.* The people at our church have given to local outreach in a most extraordinary way. We have learned that sharing specific needs for money has always resulted in not only meeting, but often exceeding, the goal. Over the past six years our budget has grown consistently in spite of building programs and recessions. We set our budget each year on faith and tell the ministries we support what we hope to give them. We have never had to send them less. Our policy is to give each ministry its support checks in person. It has made a difference for us and for them.

*Time and labor.* My motto in local missions is that "I would rather have the time and talents of one thousand people than a million dollars." If I were to really add up all the time at a dollar rate we have used to build, serve, and minister I am sure the amount would be staggering. The talents our people share is equally amazing. People tutoring young children, giving financial counseling, job training, construction advice, management training, discipleship training, medical help, emotional counseling, car and home repair, housing. It is overwhelming to think about the impact our people have had. The best thing about having people instead of money is that not only do people generate money, but they also change lives! They reproduce themselves for God's work.

*Changed lives.* I wish I could take the space to tell you about the many changed lives that this ministry has had in our church and community: the wealthy banker who has learned the true measurement of wealth, the attorney who now understands the concept of justice for the poor, and the junior-high students who have experienced poverty for a day. Local outreach ministries done right will produce changed lives for eternity.

*Community respect.* When the riots in Los Angeles started I was flooded with calls on how to give money and goods. I couldn't figure out how so many people decided to call our church. Then someone handed me a copy of the paper that listed our church as a drop-off site. Someone somewhere decided we would know what to do. That was our job. Only one other church in our immediate community was talked about. The day we went to work in Los Angeles we had ten people with us from the community! What an opportunity to share with them the "why" of our ministry. What a miracle.

*Growth in events.* We have seen our Christmas wish list explode. This is an event in which we encourage everyone to purchase an item for a specific ministry. The medical clinic will need layette sets, the men's mission may need blankets, and so forth. We stack the presents in the lobby each week during the holidays and they consistently overflow the allotted area.

Our Spring Cleaning/Auction/Talent Show raised eight thousand dollars the first year. This year, with the local economy in recession, I prayed we would just be able to hold our own. We raised over twenty thousand dollars!

We have more people from Mariners at Concrete Cowboy than kids. I have had people share their disappointment at not being able to go into Santa Ana to pick up kids for the day!

*Long-term and short-term missionaries.* We support one long-term missionary in Santa Ana. Over the years we have sent junior highers on short-term trips and supported other long-term missionaries in inner cities around the country. It is a goal of our ministry to "grow" people up from a casual involvement to lifetime service. When this happens the people of the church have the same excitement as when they send someone overseas. They pray for these people, support them, and wait to hear about God's miracles through them.

## Conclusion

If I could leave you with anything it would be this. There are so many lights in your church waiting to be used in a light show. It is your job to gather them up and in the process excite people about their value and uniqueness in living out God's heart for the poor and needy. It is also your job to arrange them in the best possible way to be most effective in creating a bright light that cannot be missed. However, it is not your job or responsibility to determine when the switch is flipped to the "on" position or when people's hearts are motivated to action. That job belongs to God and God alone. I encourage you to build a foundation for a ministry that encourages fellowship and looks for fruit. I'll be looking on the horizon for your light.

*Karen Taulien is a high-school graduate who has studied music performance, psychology, and music education in college. She served as the director of special events and Mariners Local Outreach for five years at Mariners Church, Newport Beach, California.*

## BENEVOLENCE FUND POLICIES

Purpose: The benevolence fund has been established to give financial aid to people in Mariners body who have severe financial needs.

### Guidelines for Disbursement of the Benevolence Fund

1. All requests for money from the benevolence fund will be submitted and initially evaluated by a three-member benevolence team.
2. Requests for less than $2,500.00 will be evaluated and determined by the benevolence team provided they meet at least one of the two following stipulations:
    a. Money is to meet basic necessities (food, immediate lodging, clothing or urgent medical).
    b. An urgent financial need that must be met before the Board of Elders is able to make a decision.
3. Any requests made for more than $2,500.00 or that don't meet the stipulations in point 2 will be referred to and decided by the Board of Elders. The benevolence team will evaluate any case given to the board and make a recommendation.
4. All monies distributed by the benevolence team and/or the Board of Elders will be from the benevolence fund.
5. Money given is seen as a one-time gift. A recipient may not receive aid on a regular basis. There may be extraordinary circumstances where a recipient receives a gift for a second time. (What qualifies as extraordinary circumstances will be determined by the benevolence committee.)
6. Benevolence money is a gift and not a loan. A recipient is not obligated to return or "pay back" money given to him/her. A recipient may give money to the benevolence fund at some later date if he/she desires.
7. A potential recipient must first go to family members for financial aid before he/she will be considered for benevolence money. (If a potential recipient will not go to family members for financial support there must be an adequate reason.)
8. Benevolence money is for people in the Mariners body. A potential recipient must be involved in a Mariners program on a regular basis (perhaps a period of three months or so as a minimum). Testimony of other members in the church, a local permanent address, or records of involvement in a church program may be used to check involvement.

9. Potential recipients must be willing to get counseling (financial, family, emotional, etc.) if the benevolence team and/or the Board of Elders determine personal problems led to the financial crisis. (If recommended the church will help the recipient find a good counselor.)

10. The Board of Elders or the benevolence committee has the right to refuse financial aid to anyone who, in their estimation, will have negative or irresponsible behavior reinforced by a financial gift.

11. If for any of the above reasons a person does not qualify for financial aid members of the benevolence team can assist him/her in going to the right organizations for financial aid (Welfare, FISH, etc.) and will help meeting his/her spiritual or emotional needs.

NAME _____
ADDRESS _____
CITY _____STATE _____ ZIP _____
TELEPHONE _____
AMOUNT REQUESTED _____
BRIEF SUMMARY OF NEED


PERSONAL REFERENCES AT MARINERS:
NAME _____
PHONE _____
NAME _____
PHONE _____

I have read and understand the policy of Mariners Church benevolence fund (attached). I am willing to accept this money as a gift and understand that repayment is not necessary or expected. I also am willing to accept the recommendation of the committee to enter counseling (financial or emotional) if it is deemed necessary. I understand that the committee will contact my personal references as part of determining whether or not Mariners can meet my need. It is also understood that if Mariners cannot directly meet my need there will be other options presented.

Signature of applicant _____
Signature of MLO member _____
Signature of MLO member _____

# 13

# The Inner-City
# Plunge

## *Noel Becchetti*

"Hey, man!" "Good to see you!" "God bless you!"

The greetings ring out as the men enter the large, open meeting room. There are handshakes and hugs. Everyone takes seats at tables scattered throughout the room.

Soon, the meeting begins. There are welcomes and introduction. Singing, sharing, testimonies, and passages from the Bible follow. Then, each table launches into an animated discussion on the Scripture passage selected for study.

There are several newcomers tonight, visitors from out of town. These men and women look around with varying degrees of amazement. While some are quiet, others join into the singing, sharing, and discussions.

At meeting's end, everyone stands and forms a large, joined-hands circle. Prayers are offered, especially for those facing particular trials in the week ahead. After the closing prayers, there is a little time to mingle and talk before the meeting is ended—by prison guards come to lead the inmates back to their cells.

It's another Friday night chapel service at the Cook County Jail in Chicago. The friendly greeters we heard from at the beginning of our story? Inmates awaiting trial, dressed in identical Department of Corrections khaki. The jaw-agape newcomers? Young people and adults from the suburbs, getting their first taste of the inner-city plunge.

## What Is an Inner-City Plunge?

Inner-city plunge, urban immersion, cross-cultural mission and service—there are many names given to describe it. What "it" is involves a group of people from outside a major U.S. urban city who have chosen to step across the invisible barrier from their familiar neighbors into the unknown, often terrifying "inner city."

I know these people well, because I lead these groups into their times of learning and service in Chicago with the Center for Student Missions. And I'd like you to consider taking just such a trip yourself.

Scary? Maybe. Dangerous? A lot less than you think. Valuable? If we're serious about being the church of Christ, essential.

## Why Should I Take the Plunge?

Actually, the term *inner-city plunge* is the right term for the wrong reasons. Our view of entering the city as a "plunge" reflects our common stereotype of urban centers as dark cesspools of poverty, crime, gangs, drugs, and danger.

Certainly, all of those factors exist in large cities. (And if we happen to forget, the media are kind enough to remind us—again and again and again.) But that's not the whole story. The inner cities of our nation are also full of vibrant, creative people, excitingly diverse cultures, and deliciously different foods. Most importantly, the city is full of God's people, hard at work bringing the redeeming power of the gospel to the city through local churches, rescue missions, and other organizations. It is obvious to anyone who has visited one of these institutions that they need our help—but we need theirs as well for there is much that they have to offer for our own education and development. When we step out and work alongside these men and women in the inner city, our view of God, our faith in him, and our understanding of what it means to live the Christian life is radically jolted—never to be the same. That's why we take the plunge.

The Bible is explicit in its mandate that Christians are to step out with special efforts to minister to those who are acutely impoverished, be it materially, socially, or spiritually. One of the most well-known biblical admonitions states:

> What good is it, my brothers, if a man claims to have faith but has no deeds? Can such faith save him? Suppose a brother or sister is without clothes and daily food. If one of you says to him, "Go, I wish you well; keep warm and well fed," but does nothing about his physical needs, what good is it? In the same way, faith by itself, if it is not accompanied by action, is dead. [James 2:14–17]

The first few chapters of this book illustrated the need for social action in our communities by the local body of Christ. No matter how you may interpret doctrines of Scripture, you must come to a realization that God loves people and wants the church to be involved in assisting the poor and needy. The answer to the question of *why we should take the plunge* is found in understanding the nature and unconditional love of God for mankind. In essence, we take the plunge into the inner city because God wants us to. It could be just the thing to kick your faith, and the faith of those you minister to, into overdrive.

## Breaking Through the Stereotypes

I love taking our groups to the Evangelistic Crusaders Church of God in Christ on the South Side of Chicago. When we (usually all white) arrive there (usually all African-American) for a Wednesday night or Sunday afternoon service, our groups are pleasantly surprised at the warm welcome they receive. They're impressed by the beauty of the newly rebuilt sanctuary that the church has just completed. They are flabbergasted when they discover that this newly rebuilt sanctuary was completed debt-free, through donations supplied by church members.

While groups like yours can make a real difference in the inner city, I need to remind you that you're not going to cure the ills of the inner city in a few days or a week—that would be impossible. You are there primarily to learn. And the first thing you will learn is how to break down the stereotypes you've built up about the city. As your stereotypes disappear, you will gain a vision for what God is doing in the city and you should discover some practical ways of how you can be a part of that vision.

*Stereotype 1:* The inner city is hopeless. "What can really be done about the problems of the city?" It's a common question, especially at the beginning of an inner-city plunge. Without a doubt, the problems faced in large cities are immense—chronic poverty, homelessness, poor education, family disintegration, and on and on. And I would be lying if I were to tell you that everything is going to be solved. But when God's people commit themselves to being salt and light in the inner city, great strides can be made toward improving some of these conditions.

An example of this can be found in the Jesus People U.S.A. organization here in Chicago. They have been ministering in Chicago for over twenty years. In addition to their church, they run a six-day-a-week feeding program, a day-care center, several shelters that enable women and children (the most vulnerable people among inner-city poor) to get off the street and eventually back into mainstream life, low-income housing for senior citizens, evangelistic music ministries, and a worldwide publishing ministry. They have attracted an extensive network of volunteers from all over the U.S. and the world; the collective efforts that they, and their volunteers, have made over more than two decades have made a saving difference in literally thousands of lives.

These kinds of ministries are taking on the problems of the city head-on, and making a real difference. And they could not do it without the help of volunteers like you. Believe me, your efforts are not in vain.

*Stereotype 2:* The city is too dangerous. No one needs to remind me that there are dangers in the city. I know—I live there. And yet, our misunderstanding of these dangers, fueled by the media's obsession with the sensational, can simmer our natural fears for safety into a paralyzing emotional stew.

One of the admonitions I give groups when they first arrive in Chicago is, "The first day you'll be too scared, and the second day you won't be concerned enough." That's because many people literally expect to pull up in their vans under a hail of bullets as the street gangs they envision occupy every corner of Chicago continue their never-ending shootouts. Once people get settled and say to themselves, "Well, I've been here twenty-four hours and I haven't heard a shot yet!" they can become too cavalier and not exercise reasonable caution, primarily over their possessions. Another of our slogans is, "You're safe—but your stuff isn't."

The irony for groups coming into the city from the suburbs is that they're actually safer than the residents of the neighborhoods that they visit. They're obviously not from the neighborhood; they're not part of any local gangs. If they're white (which they usually are), they can only be, as the saying goes in the city, "cops or crazy Christians." Once the neighborhood figures out that a group is not the police (and it doesn't take long), people are generally supportive of Christian groups. The basic ethos is, "Hey, if you want to come and try to help, more power to you!" People are especially impressed at the sight of teenagers who have sacrificed their time, money, and convenience to reach out to others.

The key to ministering safely in the inner city is knowing *where* to be, *when* to be there, and *who* to be with. That's where linking up with a mission organization like CSM, Jesus People U.S.A., Cambridge Institute in Boston, Habitat for Humanity, and many others can be so valuable. We know the city, and the people in it. We link you with ministry sites where you are wanted, needed, and appreciated. And most important, we know when *not* to be in certain places.

Take Ingleside, for example. It's a neighborhood on the South Side of Chicago where we've assisted with an outreach to children under the auspices of the Ingleside Church of the Nazarene. We're there virtually every day during the summer and most Saturdays during the fall, winter, and spring—during the day. Up until about 4:00 P.M., it's just about like any other neighborhood, albeit a lot poorer than most of ours. After 4:00 P.M., the gang members in the neighborhood start to come out and stake out their turf, and after 8:00 P.M., it's not a good idea to be hanging around for any reason. That's why we run all of our children's programming from 9:30 A.M. to 3:00 P.M. We're in the neighborhood when it's the right time to be there, and we're out of the neighborhood when it would be unwise to be there. It's common sense, and the people in the neighborhood understand completely. All of the law-abiding residents in the neighborhood (who are the vast majority) are already behind their doors, for the same common-sense reasons.

*Stereotype 3:* All people of color hate whites. This is the most debilitating stereotype of all, because it feeds the dark sides of racism that exist within all of us. These walls of racism contribute to our lack of understanding about people from other walks of life. I am convinced that these walls can be brought down to a lasting degree only by the miraculous power of the Holy Spirit.

That's why I love to watch our groups mingle with the inmates at the Cook County Jail at chapel. Over 80 percent of the inmates at Cook County are African-American, and most of them paint an imposing visual picture, with muscular builds and gang tattoos. To see these "frightening" men singing, sharing, laughing, and praising the Lord alongside our white men and women, boys and girls, is a powerful statement of the true nature of the body of Christ. Invariably, our groups come back awestruck at the fact that there are Christians in jail—and not just "jailhouse" Christians either. These are men who often know the wrongness of their actions and are prepared to face the consequences. Their prayer is for the Lord to keep them spiritually strong as they make their way through the harrowing life of the prison system, and then also once they have been released to the often just-as-harrowing life back on the outside. Their appreciation for the prayers and support of the volunteers who spend time with them every Friday is so tangible, you can taste it. To see men who know what it means to be "sinners saved by grace," rejoicing in God's love and mercy in such a grim setting, is a dynamic lesson in faith for our volunteers, who come to minister, yet come away feeling they are the ones who have been ministered to.

*Stereotype 4:* The church in the city is dead. One of the best reasons for experiencing an inner-city plunge is that it gives you a new look at God's church. The most common misconception we hear from people who are unfamiliar with the city is that the urban landscape is a spiritual wasteland. While there is much to mourn about how the body of Christ has addressed—or abandoned—the city, God's church is alive in the city. And these inner-city congregations often have much to teach us Anglo suburbanites about what it means to *be* a church.

Take Crusaders, for example. Not only have they rebuilt their sanctuary debt-free; they've also bought up property all around their church that they utilize in a variety of ways. They've opened a car wash that provides jobs for local residents and income for the church. They've opened Crusaders Kitchen, which provides food for needy people in their neighborhood. They manage apartment buildings that provide reasonable rents for tenants—something at a real premium in the inner city. They're not just a church on Sundays; they're involved in their community seven days a week.

This involvement has altered their community for the better. Their development projects have literally pushed back the negative forces in the neighborhood and created a peaceful zone where people can go about their business, day or night, with little to worry about. And this phenomenon is not restricted to Crusaders. Many churches in Chicago have taken the initiative to improve not only the spiritual, but also material, social, and moral environments in their neighborhoods, with dramatically visible results.

We've found that linking our groups with churches like Crusaders has a powerful effect on everyone involved. Our suburbanites get a taste, often for the first time, of what it means to be truly a *community* church. Our inner-city brethren, rather than being annoyed by these white kids piling into their services (kids who don't even know how to clap correctly!), appreciate the effort these kids and adults are making to learn about places and people different than themselves, and demonstrate impressive hospitality.

I remember the night that a group from an affluent church in Michigan was at an evening service at Crusaders. When the pastor of Crusaders learned that the group had driven over two hundred miles to get to Chicago, he had the church take an offering and presented the group with nearly one hundred dollars to help with their fuel expenses! You can imagine the impact it had on these wealthy kids and adults to be on the receiving end of such generosity from people who, by their standards, were poor. That group has never been the same since, and their church and city back in Michigan are all the better for it.

## So What Should I Do Now?

If you're ready to plan for an inner-city plunge, and you've not done one before, I highly recommend that the first thing you do is to contact one or more mission organizations whose ministry is working with church volunteers. Organizations like ours exist to link groups like yours with the best possible opportunities for inner-city mission and service, and can usually help you with logistical details that can be maddening if you're unfamiliar with the territory. You will no doubt have questions about program elements, housing transportation, and food.

When you contact these organizations, keep these questions in mind:

*What ministry opportunities do you emphasize?* Some ministries, for example, specialize in work projects, such as Habitat for Humanity. Others may emphasize people-to-people ministries, such as vacation Bible school outreaches to children, or feeding outreaches to homeless men and women. Explore the type of ministry opportunities that will play best to the needs of your group.

*How do you handle housing?* Some organizations have their own buildings; others rent apartments or rooms in inner-city residential hotels. Find out what kind of housing you'll be staying in; for example, where it's located in the city, what the surrounding neighborhoods are like. Living in the city can be a major part of your experience; don't panic if you find out that you'll be housed in the "inner city." Organizations that provide this kind of housing do so with a knowledge of the area and the common-sense rules for safety.

*How do you handle food?* Some organizations arrange for bulk food service that caters more to familiar foods. CSM intentionally contracts with local ethnic restaurants and cafes so that groups get a real taste of the various cultures that live in the inner city. We see it as a vital part of the overall experience. In any case, find out ahead of time so that you know what to expect, and what to prepare your group for.

*How do you handle leadership and supervision of my group?* Find out if you'll be provided with a "host" who stays with your group for the entire time, or if you'll be under the supervision of a coordinator who oversees several different groups. Both models can work well. Make sure you understand who is responsible for group discipline, bed checks, wake-up calls, and the like.

*How will my group process and debrief what they're experiencing?* Some organizations allow you freedom to steer these processing times as you see fit. Others provide a staff person who guides these times of discussion and reflection. Still others provide a blend of the two approaches.

*How can my group prepare for our time in the city?* Most organizations (CSM included) provide pre-trip training materials that you can use to prepare your group spiritually, socially, and mentally for their mission experience.

*Can I visit the city, and your ministry center, ahead of time?* CSM has found this component so helpful that we require a pre-visit by every group that comes into the city with us. Whether or not the organization you choose to go with requires such a visit, I cannot recommend it too highly. Make it your personal requirement, if it's not required by the mission organization. It's worth the time, effort, and expense.

# Ready, Set . . .

You may find yourself studying the Bible with prison inmates, or sharing sandwiches and punch with a new homeless friend, or painting the walls of a soon-to-be-rehabilitated home destined to be owned by a well-deserving inner-city family, or any number of other experiences. Whatever the particulars of your inner-city plunge, I can guarantee that you, and your group, will not return home the same. Discovering the inner city, meeting its people, celebrating their delights and sharing their struggles, and being a part of what God is about with his people in the urban centers of North America will change the way you understand, and live, your Christian life. It could very well change the vocational course of your own life. And it will revitalize your congregation, and give it a renewed appetite for sacrificial ministry and service right in its neighborhood and communities that can be appropriated in no other way. That's my promise; you can take it to the bank.

See you in the city!

*Noel Becchetti is director of ministries for the Center for Student Missions. Based in Chicago, he oversees the ministries of CSM's Chicago, Los Angeles, and Washington, D.C. ministry centers. Previous to his move to CSM in May 1992, Noel served full-time as vice president, publishing, for Youth Specialties in El Cajon, California. Noel continues to direct Youth Specialties' publishing operations on a part-time basis in addition to his responsibilities with CSM.*

# 14

# The Sidewalk Sunday School

## *Bill Wilson and Chris Blake*

America has a problem it refuses to face. Unless there is a revolution in the basic education of our children, this nation will crumble from within. Our demise will not come from an economic collapse, but from a moral bankruptcy—and it is well on its way.

Problems once unique to the inner city are now common in most suburbs as well. Drug dealing, gang violence, AIDS, teenage pregnancy, prostitution, and child neglect were, at one time, the exclusive domain of the urban landscape. Today, as we near the end of the twentieth century, these problems have invaded Everytown, U.S.A.

There must be a solution. We cannot afford to throw our next generation away. We certainly can't wait for the government to find a solution. Our government has become the golden calf of our churches. There was a time when the church took responsibility for the social problems of our society. We educated future leaders, we fed the hungry, we sheltered the homeless, we cared for unwed mothers, and we provided for the orphans. Why? Because it was our biblical mandate. Today, instead of looking to God to help us meet these overwhelming needs, we simply wait for the government to design and implement a new program.

## Lighting Up Our World

The responsibility must be laid squarely on the shoulders of the church. So where do we begin? First of all, let's realize that the problems we face are not too big for God. Even though the problems seem hopeless and the sins that caused the problems seem embedded in our society, the Bible teaches that where sin abounds grace does much more abound. It takes only a little light to dispel the darkness, and God has called us, his church, to be the bearers of that light. It reminds me of a boy who lived near one of our Sidewalk Sunday School sites in Harlem. The little boy lived on 126th Street, and day after day he took a little piece of a broken mirror and reflected beams of light up to an apartment in a tenement house. "What do you think you are doing?" asked a policeman who had been watching the boy for several days. "Are you bothering those people up there?"

"No, sir," said the little boy. "That apartment is where I live."

"Then why are you shining that light up there?" the policeman wanted to know. "Well, mister, that is where my little brother is. He is six years old and has never been able to walk. My mother doesn't have enough money to buy a wheelchair. If we bring him outside and carry him, the kids make fun of him. He doesn't want to come down. So every day I stand here and try to shine some light into his room, because that is the only light he sees."

That little bit of light made all the difference in the world for that six-year-old boy. How much more does God's light make a difference in the lives of those that everyone else has given up on. God's light can make a difference, but someone has to take the light where it's most needed.

## God Always Calls People

Denominations and institutions have their place, but as we look historically at how God intervenes in the life of a nation we discover that God always calls a man or a woman. To effect the magnitude of change that is needed we have to realize that it depends on us— you and I. We are the ones who will make the difference. I think we can all agree that this next generation is the critical one. If we lose this generation, I'm afraid we will lose our country. Yet how do you reach a generation? You reach it one child at a time. Christianity was never a religion. It was, and is, built on relationships. That's where you and I come in. I'm not D. L. Moody, and I'm not as famous as Billy Graham and neither are you. I don't preach like Billy Sunday. As a matter of fact, of all the great men, I feel more like Edward Kimball. What, you've never heard of him? Well, if it weren't for Edward Kimball none of those men I mentioned would be in the ministry.

Mr. Kimball was a shoe salesman in Massachusetts. He taught Sunday school every Sunday. God had called him to work with the boys in his hometown. One day he got up enough courage to talk to a young boy about Christ. That young boy's name was Dwight. Twenty-one years later Dwight Lyman Moody won to the Lord a young man by the name of F. B. Meyer, who also grew up to be a preacher. An avid enthusiast of personal visitation, Meyer won a young man by the name of J. W. Chapman to Christ. Chapman in turn grew up to be a preacher and brought the message of Christ to a baseball player named Billy Sunday. As an athlete/evangelist, Sunday held a revival in Charlotte, North Carolina, that was so successful that another evangelist by the name of Mordecai Hamm was invited to Charlotte to preach. It was while Hamm was preaching that a teenager named Billy Graham gave his life to Jesus. It all started with a shoe salesman who took the time to develop a relationship with a young boy. Where are the Ed Kimballs today?

Our ministry is in the toughest ghettoes of New York City. We have a motto that serves as the foundation for all that we do. It reads, "It's easier to build boys and girls than it is to repair men and women." Statistics tell us that 85 percent of the people who are saved, were saved before they were sixteen years old. Yet most ministry to young people is relegated to the back rooms and basements of our churches. I doubt that this will change until a change in thinking occurs. This paradigm shift will happen as more and more people begin ministering to the next generation of the church on a one-on-one basis. It has been said that "no child would ever turn out bad if he or she had just one person who really cared and took a personal interest in him or her."

## The Need Is the Call

Many believers have accepted the notion that God has a "perfect will for their lives." The problem with this concept is that this elusive will is always spoken of in the future sense. When they find it they will be at peace. Their problems will have been laid to rest, and life will be wonderful. For some it is finding God's chosen mate for them; for others it is a place to live. Still others see this perfect will as a new job that God will reveal to them any day. Relatively few Christians testify about experiencing this perfect will. The real problem with this concept is that it is not scriptural.

Those who buy into this theology get consumed in living for the future. They live their lives with little regard for today because life becomes one long search. Since there is no sure way of knowing whether what you have found is God's perfect will, life becomes a long search. I prefer to believe that God's will is closer to most believers than they care to realize.

If you see a need today, and you can fill that need, then that's God's will for your life today. If you do that today and tomorrow and the next day and every day, you will find yourself so deep in the will of God that you will have a hard time getting out even if you wanted to. In a real sense, the need becomes the call. Look around you today. Look at the children and the families that God has put all around you. Look at their needs. Do you know what you are looking at? The call of God on your life. Everyone can answer the call. It's up to you whether or not you will.

## Whose Child Is This?

Maybe you can't do something that would change our society as a whole. You can do something to change it for one child. Hundreds of the children we deal with are born into families in which love has somehow been lost. That is the story of Danny. One morning when he was only three, Danny was sitting in his crib with his legs sticking out of the side slats. His mother, infuriated by his crying, jerked up on the side of his crib, and both of his tiny legs were broken. The physical abuse did not stop. Doctors say his mild case of cerebral palsy is a direct result of a severe blow to his head which he suffered as a young child.

At the age of eleven Danny took matters into his own hands. He ran away from home and spent two days riding the subways. When he was exhausted, he found his way back home. His mother was waiting for him with a two-by-four.

It was during this time that a volunteer from our church knocked on the door of his apartment and invited him to ride the bus to Sunday school. She said, "Jesus loves you, and I love you too!" and she gave him a big hug. Danny was not used to hugs. He decided to come to Sunday school because "that lady talked about love and I wanted some." He became a familiar face at church.

Today more than half the kids in Danny's neighborhood are in jail or addicted to drugs. But Danny found a way out. He works in the Sidewalk Sunday School Department here at Metro Church. Every week he goes to Harlem and shares with hundreds of children. He shares with children just like himself. He shares a love that changed his life.

How many kids are there like Danny in your neighborhood? How many need someone to tell them they love them?

What we are talking about is obviously more than having church. It goes beyond the realm of the Sunday morning worship service with the occasional visitor. It is about changing a generation. I have to emphasize that it is more than reaching kids or boosting your church attendance. The future of our country is hanging in the balance. Whose child is this? This child is ours.

## Testing Our Theology: The Sidewalk Sunday School

The most effective tool we have found is a relatively new idea called Sidewalk Sunday School. The whole concept started in our ministry in the early 1980s. It was at that point we realized that, although we were reaching thousands of inner-city kids on the streets of Brooklyn every week, there was no way we could continue to grow. We had reached our capacity on the buses and in our building. The problem was that we knew there were still hundreds of thousands of children all over New York City that needed to be reached.

The philosophy was born in the idea that instead of bringing the masses to our Sunday school, we would take our Sunday school to them. This program has since spread around the world. It has been improved on and duplicated, but that underlying philosophy has remained unchanged.

We believe that the church is not the building—the church is the people of God. Though the theology of that statement may seem simple to state, translating that theology into the simplicity of getting out on the streets takes a good deal of creative thinking. We decided to put our theology to the test and take the service outside. We took a truck, cut the side out of it, and used that for a fold-down stage. We loaded the truck with all of our equipment and faithfully went back to the same location every week. In time, we developed a congregation that met outside.

We stretched out theology a little more by asking, "Does the church have to meet only on Sundays?" It would certainly be more economical to use the same truck at different locales on different days of the week. We found that if we tried to have adult services outside, the adults tended to be intimidated. In fact, we found out that they wouldn't show up. So we rethought our strategy and geared the first part of our program exclusively to children. As a result, not only did we get a large group of children, but the parents also came out. We found that the easiest way to get a large group of parents was to have a program for a large group of kids. The parents would naturally come out, because the nature of the program is nonthreatening. At present, we have thirty of these Sidewalk Sunday School congregations meeting all over New York City. The number that have started all over the world, in urban, suburban, and rural settings is far too many to count.

Sidewalk Sunday School is an updated version of the old Neighborhood Bible Club idea. But this new format is so powerful that we believe it could spearhead a modern-day revival. It is inexpensive to operate and is applicable to every town and city in America. But what about all the problems that come with it? Do the kids come when there are so many other things vying for their attention? What about the weather? Where we live it's too hot (or cold or rainy). What if you don't have permission? How do you get workers? The list of problems goes on forever. It seems like the list of reasons not to do it is endless. Let me share a few of the practical steps to take to make it happen.

# What Does It Take to Start?

What does it take to start a Sidewalk Sunday School? You need committed people. Here in New York, where the program is a major part of our church, we have several trucks that go out six days a week, run by full-time staff with a large budget to back them up. But don't let the size of our ministry discourage you. We started with one volunteer going out with the church van once a week, and the ministry has grown and evolved from there.

We use old fourteen-foot cube vans that have stages that sit about four feet off the ground and have been customized to suit our needs. They are big because we found that when we go into an inner-city area we want to attract as much attention as possible. In New York, where we minister, large populations of people live in relatively small neighborhoods. In essence, we deal with crowds of people. For our ministry to be effective we need to have a stage that is high enough to be seen by everyone. The vehicles are modified to meet our unique ministry needs but what works for us here may not be well suited for your needs.

In your ministry locale you may not need a large truck. One of our branch Sunday schools in St. Louis came up with the unique concept of fully-equipped trailers that can be pulled behind any vehicle with a trailer hitch. Some churches that have replicated the Sidewalk Sunday School program have used an old church school bus with a table set up in front as a stage. It works for them and that's what counts. In fact, when one of our large trucks has a mechanical breakdown, we will transfer some of the supplies into a church van and use it for the same purpose.

The Sidewalk Sunday School program has also been replicated in foreign countries. Once, when I was ministering in a foreign country, we had a difficult time finding and maintaining a large truck so we went with a Chevy Chevette instead. Talk about improvising! It worked. You can use anything. The most important thing is that you get your people and your supplies to the neighborhoods where they are needed.

# What about Staff?

What qualifications do you look for when trying to find someone to run a Sidewalk Sunday School site? Several things come to mind.

First, you need people who have a desire to minister to the poor and needy of our inner city with an attitude of servanthood. Secondly, staff must be committed for the long haul, which means they need a degree of faithfulness. Inner-city children and youth have grown up with parents, especially fathers, who come and go with little concern for commitment. The church needs to demonstrate something different. Lastly, you need at least some staff with talent. They don't have to be professional singers, preachers, or counselors, but the more training they have in these areas the more effective the program will become. Find a balance between those who are qualified by their willingness to serve and those who are qualified by their talents. Both are needed.

## Program Format

The Sidewalk Sunday School ministry is unique because it is geared toward the needs of children. The first half-hour is filled with songs and games. The children sit on tarps in front of the stage and are enthralled because the first part of the program is exciting. There isn't a moment of dead time. They can't imagine a more fun or exciting place to be. So you need people who are excited about working with children—high-energy people with a contagious personality and vivacious spirit. However, it doesn't stop there.

After the first half-hour of enthusiastic music you must take a few minutes to calm the children down. You make a transition into a time of teaching and presentation of the gospel message. You must not shy away from the heart of the program: the declaration of God's remedy for lost man. The games and songs are fun, the contests and prizes are exciting, but none of those things can change lives. Only the presentation of God's Word can do that.

Keep the presentation of the gospel simple. Remember that there will be a broad spectrum of age levels present and their attention span will be short. In addition, the gospel presentation must be visual. Statistics tell us that 83 percent of everything we learn, we learn through our eyes.

The gospel presentation must also be focused. We have only one point or theme that we are trying to drive home. Our Scripture memory verse, our Bible lesson, our object lessons, and our main story are all focused on the same theme.

Keep in mind that you are not speaking just to the children but also to the multitude of parents who have gathered at the back of the crowd. The fun and exciting part of the program is not an end unto itself. It is there by design. We use it to draw a crowd. Not only do the parents come out to watch over their children, but also they come out because of the festive atmosphere that our program creates. They will be listening to your message too. Don't treat them like spectators of the program but present the gospel to them as well. We consider this to be one of the most important elements of our program.

When we get to the end of the gospel presentation we include an altar call in our program, and we have the altar call right there in the street. We have the adults walk the aisle with their children. When you see parents and children coming forward to accept the healing that only God can give their lives, at that moment you realize the investment of your ministry resources.

## What Does It Cost?

The money you set aside for the Sidewalk Sunday School can be one of the biggest expenses in your budget, or it can be free. I think it goes without saying that the more you invest, the bigger return you will see. Obviously you will need some form of liability insurance, but you can reach more people with less insurance money than you can with a large bus ministry. (See chapter 8 for a discussion on church liability insurance issues.) It would be a good idea to have any minors working in the program have medical and liability release forms signed by their parents or legal guardians. Prizes and promotions are a consideration, too. However, many times these items can be purchased at a discount rate or acquired from a local business as a donation. Creativity is always a key to coming up with funds and materials needed on a small budget.

## Visitation: Consistency Is the Key to Success

Finally, I want to stress the importance of a strong, consistent visitation program. Our Sunday school is averaging over fourteen thousand in weekly attendance. Many people ask us what is the secret for the high numbers. Our staff is composed of over fifty full-time peo-

ple and two hundred and fifty volunteers who make more than sixteen thousand personal visits to these kids every week. What we have
done is taken the different parts of the city that we are working in and
divided them up into smaller sections. Every volunteer, worker, and
helper has a section that they call their own. They saturate that area
every week, visiting the children who attend and their families. They
also work hard at signing up new children. Most of the calls are simple one-minute visits that remind the children and their parents
about church and what is going on that week. We want to establish
a presence in their communities and let them know that we care
enough to come to their home. Here are a few reasons why a consistent visitation program works:

1. Personal visitation programs place workers in the world of the
children they seek to reach. The Bible states that God so loved the
world that he sent his Son. God felt that visitation was an essential
component of his ministry to mankind, so it serves as a foundation
for ours as well. The time has come for the church to get out of the
church and back into the world.

2. Personal visitation establishes a person-to-person relationship.
This one factor alone would eliminate probably 80 percent of the discipline problems that the average public school teacher faces in the
classroom. Once you gain a person's respect he or she will listen to
what you have to say.

3. Personal visitation prevents alienation. Many Christian leaders
have lost touch with the needs of their congregations because they
no longer take the time to visit them in their homes and community
settings. There was a time when such approaches to ministry were
common. It has now become more the exception than the norm for
a pastor to do personal visitation. This neglect can alienate the leader
from the real needs of the people.

4. Personal visitation prepares personalities. By being personally
involved with these children's families and their day-to-day lives,
you can minister to them and see them grow in ways that you would
have never dreamed possible by just "having church."

5. Personal visitation promotes productivity. Beyond any shadow
of doubt, the greatest way to see your church grow is by a strong visitation and soul-winning program. There is no telling where your
church will be if people catch the vision for it.

6. Personal visitation projects an image of your ministry. What image is your church projecting in your community? Any? It would have been impossible for our ministry in New York to have accomplished what it has without the power of our visitation program. We have taken God to the people and they have responded. Many people think that because our ministry reaches so many thousands that we are "only interested in numbers." Nothing could be farther from the truth. I constantly tell our workers that the numbers that they bring in are worthless unless they represent relationships that they have built. I have heard far too many professional ministry leaders say that they would rather choose quality over quantity any day. To me, that is just an excuse for being lazy. I believe it is possible to have both.

## Conclusion

North Americans contribute 90 percent of all the money that goes to help foreign missions. Foreign missions is important. However, in the process of reaching out to those of other cultures we must not neglect the mission field within our own borders. A major shift of emphasis needs to occur if we are to bring our country back from the brink of moral, social, and spiritual destruction.

We haven't lost our nation yet. The battle for America's children and youth is still being waged each week. Every week our national media emblazon headlines that rivet our attention on problems that are besetting our country. But they *never* offer solutions. To me, the solution is obvious. "And the Lord said unto the servant, 'Go out into the highways and hedges and compel them to come in, that my house may be filled.'"

There are over six billion people currently living on the face of the earth. They all arrived on this planet the same way. They came one at a time. The church in America must not allow itself to become discouraged by the magnitude of the challenge before it. We must mobilize to reach our lost and needy children with the message of hope and salvation in Christ. Different methods are needed for different community needs. The Sidewalk Sunday School program has been one very successful program that has contributed to bringing the lost and needy into the family of God in many cities around America and in other countries around the world. It is our hope that it may be an effective ministry tool for your church as well.

*Bill Wilson is the founder and senior pastor of Metro Assemblies of God in Brooklyn, New York. He oversees over sixty full-time staff and hundreds of volunteers. After twenty-five years of experience in the inner city, Wilson's Bible-based concepts are serving as a working model for inner-city and suburban outreach programs throughout America and abroad.*

*Chris Blake is the Sunday school director of Metro Assemblies of God. Over fourteen thousand inner-city children attend Metro's unique Sunday school program on a weekly basis. Drawing on his experience as the director of the largest children's ministry in North America, Blake leads workshops and seminars in developing inner-city ministries for children. He writes for and teaches America's toughest audience every week.*

# 15

# Come Play for a Day: Activities for the Disadvantaged

## *Pam Reed Allison*

Planning a community outreach program in a local church for the first time can be intimidating. It takes time, commitment, and a lot of hard work. However, I can almost guarantee that the outcome will be rewarding. Not only will you see results in the lives of those you are serving, but you will see a change in many of your church members, too.

Normally, churches get involved in the community to bring relief to those who are less fortunate and in need. And there is good reason to do so. The Census Bureau estimates that 14.2 percent of the U.S. population lived under the poverty line in 1991. Even more frightening was the report that 21.8 percent of the children in this country lived in poverty. We no longer have to look at Third-World nations to see starvation. It is in our own backyard! Most of our local churches have the resources to help bring some relief, and many are willing to get involved. They need to know where to start.

This chapter is intended to provide some tips on how to plan an all-day outreach program to your community. First, it will give you ideas on how to get your church volunteers interested in participating in such a project. I have learned from experience that if your church members are not interested, even with the best intentions, you may become quickly frustrated and eventually give up. Second, it will provide you with a step-by-step guide for organizing, administering, and implementing the program.

The chapter will emphasize an outreach program I had the privilege of organizing while I was a student at Biola University. The program was called "Come Play for a Day" and was designed to get our students involved in meeting the needs of the underprivileged near our campus community. It may be something your church would like to replicate, or it may be that you have already recognized a community to target. These guidelines should help you to get such a program off the ground.

## Phase I: Getting Started

*Step 1: Select a leader.* If you are thinking about starting an outreach program, the first thing you have to do is decide who will plan it. Most senior pastors do not have the time to administer such a project. The logical choice in a large church would be an assistant pastor or a missions coordinator. However, most churches have a more limited staff. If this is your case, you may need to delegate the project to a deacon, an elder, or a parishioner who has administrative skills and a vision to serve others.

*Step 2: Select a community.* Once you know who will spearhead the program, you will then need to decide what type of program you will organize. You may already know. It may be that you pass a park inhabited by homeless people every day on your way to work and you feel a burden to help those individuals. If you already feel drawn to a particular community, I would suggest targeting it. But chances are that you have not yet narrowed your focus. If this is the case, assess the needs of the community around your church. I believe the myth of missions is that you must go far away in order to "do ministry."

Don't get caught up in the idea that you have to go to an area such as South Central Los Angeles in order to minister. The truth is, there are needs everywhere—even in affluent areas. Pain and poverty are all around you; they might be hidden.

As a student at Biola University, I experienced this first-hand. Biola is a Christian college located in Southern California, on the border of Orange and Los Angeles counties. Everyone knows of the problems in Los Angeles—South Central has been overtaken by gangs, crime, and poverty. Orange County, on the other hand, is one of the wealthiest areas of the country. It is a virtual paradise, or so one would think. Class differences are not apparent. However, well hidden just ten miles down the road from Biola, an apartment community houses large families of Cambodian and Laotian refugees, many of whom narrowly escaped death during the Vietnam War. These families are crowded into one- and two-bedroom rundown apartments. They are desperately trying to make ends meet. On any given day, one could walk down the street and see literally hundreds of children sitting in the dirt-filled courtyards with nothing to do. While most of us knew the problems in our society were widespread, we never realized they were actually staring us in the face.

I became involved in organizing an outreach program to these children through my work in student government. The board under which I served was responsible for community outreach, and the year before I became involved it had held for the first time a program for the children in this Orange County "ghetto." We named the program "Come Play for a Day" and set a goal to take what had been done previously and expand it into a regular monthly activity. With the hard work of a small group of dedicated students, within a year we had achieved our goal.

*Step 3: Make contact with the community.* If you are not sure of the needs in the community surrounding your church, do some investigating. You may wish to contact your local city or county government's human services department and ask them to define areas that are underserved. Or contact a local charity, such as a homeless shelter or the Kiwanis Club. These organizations may have a service project of their own in which you can become involved, or they can be a great resource or referral source to needs that are currently going unmet.

Before you start planning your outreach, make sure you have approval from the appropriate people. In the case of "Come Play for a

Day," we felt it was important to receive permission from the land-lord to run the program, as we were in essence trespassing on his property. In some cases, however, this may not be necessary. If you are planning a day-long program with homeless in the park, there probably is no one to ask. However, you might want to contact the parks and recreation department for approval.

You may also want to do some research to make sure the community you are considering is not already served by another church or charitable organization. This does not mean you should search for another area, but you might wish to coordinate your plans with the other organization so your efforts are not duplicated.

*Step 5: Mobilize your congregation.* Once you have decided on a tar-get area, you must begin to get the congregation interested. Do not assume that because you have the vision, everyone else will too. It is possible that many in your church have no idea that needs exist. It is your job to educate them. Ask you pastor for time during a service to introduce the program. Explain what needs you have seen. Perhaps you can show some slides depicting the needs. At this point, it is not necessary to have planned all of the specifics of the program. But by introducing the issues to your church members, and illustrating the distress in the community, you can help spark their interest.

You may need to exhort. I certainly do not believe that everyone must have the same concerns, but I do think Christ has commanded each of us to serve those less fortunate than ourselves. In churches located in more affluent areas, it may require you to challenge the comfort zone. I have a friend who is on staff at a large church in Or-ange County. It is a fairly wealthy congregation, and from what I have been told, most of the people are very generous. However, liv-ing in an area where needs are less obvious, the church had literally no social outreach.

My friend got a little impassioned after reading in the church bul-letin that the women in the congregation were getting together to "do their colors." If you are not familiar with this activity, it is a fashion theory (which is probably accurate) that all people have a "season" of clothing colors in which they look their best, and seminars are held to determine this. Several weeks after the activity was held, my friend was scheduled to speak at a dinner honoring new members joining the church. He took the opportunity to talk about service. After spending some time outlining what he felt was the biblical definition of service, my friend closed his Bible and concluded by saying that their church is not one in which a poor single mother would find refuge, because she has no need for "doing her colors." And he sat down.

Much to my friend's surprise, he did not lose his job. In fact, while he was out of town for several weeks, the church started a soup kitchen for the homeless. While I would not necessarily suggest taking the same approach, this example shows how you may need to challenge your congregation a little more than you would prefer. People get comfortable, and it may be up to you to push them to get involved.

During your announcement, explain your vision and ask for volunteers to help you coordinate the program. Two heads are always better than one, and putting ten together can create quite a brainstorming session.

## Phase 2: Planning and Organizing the Program

Once you have laid some of the groundwork, you move into a second phase of program development. The goal of this second phase is to begin adding structure, organization, and detail to your plans.

*Step 1: Develop a preliminary plan.* Once you have the support of the congregation and a small network of volunteers, you can begin planning the specifics of the program itself. Meet several times with your volunteers. I suggest taking them to the community you plan to target. When I first started planning "Come Play for a Day," the board chair and I took our staff of ten to the apartment complex to see the problems of the community. We felt that if the board members saw the poverty, they would internalize the problems and work harder to get other students to participate in the project. It will help for your volunteers to see the needs so they can understand what is required to help fulfill them. After doing so, you should then sit down with your volunteers to start developing a preliminary plan for the program.

The key is to start small. Rarely will you find a large successful program that has not been grown from something smaller. My life dream is to one day start a community center in a needy community. This center would include a soup kitchen, a co-op market, a homeless shelter, a thrift shop, a job-training (computer literacy) program, a life-skills training program, and who knows what else. Could you imagine if I decided one day to open this? Realistically, I know the center must start with one component, the soup kitchen for instance, and over many years could possibly grow into my dream. If you set small, realistic goals, you will have a much better chance of seeing your program grow.

This was true for "Come Play for a Day." As a student leader, I worked to take a program that was held once the previous year and expanded it to a once-a-semester project. The following year, we held two large day-long programs each semester as well as smaller outreach days each month. We also worked with our student missions organization to have some students go weekly and tutor some of the children as fulfillment of Biola's Christian service requirement. Hold on to your vision and God will grow your program in his time.

*Step 2: Financing your program.* Once you have decided the community on which to focus, and have developed a preliminary plan regarding the specifics of the program itself, you should begin investigating the finances available from your church budget to assist with the program. In order to know how much money or resources you need, you should think about what your preliminary program will entail in terms of human and material resources. For instance, do you want this to be a one-time event, as was "Come Play for a Day" initially, or do you envision it to be a regular (e.g., weekly, monthly) activity? Be realistic. If interest in the program is low to begin with, holding the activity on a weekly basis probably is not wise.

Discuss with your pastor the amount of money the church can provide for the event. Your church may already have a fund established for outreach or for meeting needs in the community. If it does not, find out if there are any funds available. You will need to take this into consideration when deciding how extensive you will make the event. It may be wise to submit a proposed budget to your pastor. He or she may be more receptive if you have specified the funds you need. If you are considering a large project that will require a substantial amount of resources, I suggest making more than one budget. Draft one proposed budget that will include all aspects of the large project. But you may also want to scale down the project with a smaller budget in case the pastor feels your first estimate is too high.

Do not be discouraged if the money the church gives you is a small amount. There are other ways to acquire resources. Churches are great at fundraising. First, discuss with your pastor the possibility of starting a fund drive. The church I attend has designated the second Sunday of the month as "Hunger Sunday." In addition to our regular offerings, we have the opportunity to give additional money to the hunger fund, which is used to feed those in the community. Of course, if an additional offering is not an option, there is always the old church stand-by—the car wash! Be creative. There are many ways to raise money.

Many churches also collect food, and if you are planning to hold any type of feeding project, I suggest implementing some type of collection. My favorite method for collecting food at a church is to do it during the regular offering—weekly or monthly—and have the children in the church bring food forward and place it in a basket. Some churches even encourage their parishioners to have their children do a specific chore each week to earn money to purchase the food. The kids feel a sort of ownership of the project if they are the ones picking out and paying for the food. It is a great way to teach children that there are many people less fortunate than they, and that they have the ability to help. You can also set a collection box in the narthex and invite people to bring food whenever they can.

*Step 3: Develop a schedule for the event.* Now that you have your target community and know how extensive your program will be, there are many other specifics on which to focus. You must decide what will happen during the program. Start thinking about a schedule. Whether your project is narrowly focused or broad, it is imperative that you develop a schedule. If you decide on something broad, you will realize the need for having the congregation behind the program.

The "Come Play for a Day" project gave Biola students the opportunity to travel to an apartment complex and play for several hours a day with the kids. In order to provide a variety of activities for the children, we tapped into the many skills of students. We contacted the Intramurals Board chair and had him arrange all the sporting events and bring the equipment. He organized softball, football, and basketball games with the children. Our Associated Student president played the guitar, so we asked him to lead singing. We had resident assistants from the dorms bring butcher paper the school gave them to make hall signs, and had them arrange for the women on their floors to bring crayons. Once we arrived, we rolled out the paper along the sidewalk for several hundred feet and sat and colored with the children for hours. For those kids not interested in sports, we played "London Bridge," "Red Rover," "Duck, Duck, Goose," and other children's games. We had also arranged with the Biola cafeteria to bring fruit, cookies, and punch. And at the end of the day, while the kids ate, Biola's resident juggler performed for them, and the A. S. president led singing.

We were able to arrange such a full day of activity because of the diverse gifts the students possessed. You should also take advantage of the diversity in your congregation. Many churches today do a "gifts" or skills assessment survey to help determine where each member can best serve. If this has already been done, ask your pastor if you could look through the surveys. If your church has not conducted such a survey, ask the pastor for permission to do so yourself. Insert in a bulletin one Sunday a short questionnaire that asks about each individual's talents. Include questions about vocation, hobbies, and interests. You pastor may be able to give you a sample, or you can always find one in Christian education curricula.

After the surveys are completed, contact those who have skills you need. Do not feel embarrassed to call someone who did not volunteer when you made the initial announcement. We did not wait for students to contact us about being involved with "Come Play for a Day." We thought the Intramurals Board chair was the most logical person to arrange the sports activities, so we asked him to do so. Unless someone is genuinely too busy or has no interest, chances are that person will be willing to help if he or she feels needed. If you are planning to feed the homeless, contact the people in your congregation you know have great recipes. If you want to hold a job training or literacy program, contact the teachers and/or computer experts in the church. Some people might have minivans and would be willing to drive others to the location you are holding your event. You will be amazed at the talents with which some people are blessed.

Determine when and where your first activity will be held, including its duration. Make a schedule and plug in the volunteers. Put one person in charge of each aspect of the day. With the "Come Play for a Day" project, I had hardly any responsibilities the entire day because I had delegated the tasks to others. If you take time to organize, the program should run itself. You will need to be there to make sure things run smoothly and, of course, have fun.

*Step 4: Begin training.* After you have your financing arranged and know what the project will entail, you should then hold a training session for those participating. The complexity of the program will determine how long and involved you must make the training session.

You will first need to educate those participating in the project about the community to be served. Taking your volunteers to the site can help. However, if you have a large group, as we did at Biola, it is not realistic to do so. But there are many other ways to facilitate training. The easiest way is to bring in someone who knows the community. The first time we held "Come Play for a Day," I met several times with the woman who planned the program the year before and absorbed all I could about the community. The day of the event, we sat down with all the students who showed up and explained what they were about to encounter. Discuss any safety problems there may be in the area. While safety was not much of an issue at that apartment complex four years ago, I knew that gangs had organized in the area since then. If there are similar concerns in your community, you will need to prepare for them.

You should then review the details of the program and assign responsibilities to newcomers. Go through the schedule of the day's events. Outline the timetable for each activity. As with "Come Play for a Day," in order to ensure that each activity can fit into the day's agenda, you will need each person to understand and facilitate the events. Before leaving campus, we explained each aspect of the day's event. Those individuals who have not yet been assigned to a task should be given one before arriving at the location. This was something important with Biola's project. For instance, the Intramurals Board chair discussed all the sports activities he was holding and asked for volunteers to run each one. While some activities were spontaneously begun, it helped to have each person know his or her responsibilities before arriving at the complex.

*Step 5: Advertise the event.* When all details are secure and the project completely arranged, think about advertising. It may or may not require much effort, but it is nevertheless important. Several days before "Come Play for a Day," we went to the apartment complex and passed out flyers to let the children know we were coming. You should do the same. Go to the area and pass out flyers, talk to people,

and alert them to what you are planning. Otherwise, you may organize a fun-filled day, bring many volunteers, but arrive at the location
to find no one there.

## Phase 3: The Day of the Event

The day of the event (particularly if it is your first time holding
such an event) will undoubtedly be hectic. Even if you are the strongest administrator in the world, things will probably go wrong. It
may be, as happened at Biola, that more people show up than have
cars and you have to face something you had not thought much
about—transportation. You cannot plan on the little things that go
wrong. But do not panic. If you do not act like there is anything
wrong, most people will not even know. Stay calm and solve any
problems as they arise.

When you get to the site, make sure you help get things off the
ground. Even though your volunteers will know their responsibilities, they may still be a little nervous about doing something for the
first time. When we arrived the first time we had to face several obstacles. First, those who were running the sports activities did not
know where to go to play the games as they were not familiar with
the area. Because I had been to the complex several times, I knew the
layout of the area and could quickly point them to the back of the
apartments, where one of the large courtyards was used for football
and the other for baseball.

Our second obstacle was even more of a problem . . . no kids
showed up! Even though we had taken our board members to the
area several days before and passed out flyers letting the kids know
we were coming, I would say only ten were waiting for us when we
got there. We panicked for a few seconds, but then asked the board
members to walk up and down the streets gathering more children.
By an hour into the program, we had between two and three hundred children playing with us. Reflecting back, we should have had
our flyers translated into Vietnamese. This is something to keep in
mind if your program targets a multiethnic area.

The third and somewhat comical obstacle came toward the end of
the day. During the singing and entertainment portion of the day, we
also passed out fruit, cookies, and punch to the children. Trying to
get two hundred hungry children to take only one piece of fruit and

two cookies was a difficult task at best. We had to assemble about half our volunteers just to monitor the food distribution. It was next to impossible because we did not know who had come through the line already, and although we laughed at our attempt to police these kids, to be fair to everyone, we had to try. We got caught off guard by their enthusiasm and determination.

Expect things like that to happen because they undoubtedly will. But if you have organized the day with a thought-out schedule, your obstacles will be minimal. Take the opportunity to walk around and make sure there are no problems. You should be the problem solver and program overseer, not an activity facilitator. When the day is over, you and your volunteers will feel good about the accomplishments and will be willing to do it again. The stress level will be low and memories golden if the program is well organized.

## Conclusion

Anyone can organize a day-long outreach program. All it takes is vision and determination. If this is a task you are considering, take a risk and try it. It may or may not be something for which your congregation is prepared, but unless you take initiative and approach the subject, you will never know if they are willing to be involved. It requires time and dedication, so if you already have your plate full, find someone else to oversee the project. If you want to see a project like this continue, you must devote a significant amount of time and energy.

Most importantly, you need to pray. I believe the poor, the underclass, and the marginalized have a special place in God's plan. Throughout Scripture his people are commanded to care for the poor, the widows, and the orphans. Continually ask for his guidance, wisdom, and strength as you prepare to minister to the needy in your midst.

*Pam Reed Allison graduated from Biola in 1990 with a degree in Christian education. While a student at Biola she was the student director of "Come Play for a Day." She recently worked for the State Department in Washington, D.C., and now lives in southern California.*

# 16

# Conducting a World Hunger Day at Your Church

## *Todd Alexander*

You are probably familiar with the old story about the chicken and the pig. One day they were talking about doing something special for the farmer's birthday. "I know," said the chicken, "we'll make him breakfast!"

"What will we make?" asked the pig.

"Bacon and eggs!" came the chicken's reply.

"Don't get me wrong," said the pig. "It's a nice idea but while your part requires a contribution, my part requires ultimate sacrifice!"

It's an amusing story but one with a good point. Before we ask people to do something, we had better know what we want to accomplish and consider what we're asking them to do. In this chapter we'll be presenting some ideas that you can use with your church or school or other type of group. The ideas are interesting, and possibly even good, but ideas are far more effective when employed as part of a strategy.

Please take the opportunity to learn from my mistakes. For a long time I made the error of thinking that if I focused on raising people's awareness, ultimately it would rise to a point where their behavior would change. I spent many hours preparing messages, creating charts and graphs, writing articles, and conducting programs designed to give people information about missions and world hunger. The idea was that they would eventually see or hear enough and be motivated to do something. Wrong! Information is important and useful, but there is no guarantee that any amount of information, no matter how effectively it is presented, will produce long-term impact and change in the recipients.

I now see that sharing information is only the first step in a process. The process is one that people go through when they make a change in the way they look at the world and live their lives. The goal of the first step is to raise awareness, and we use information as the means to accomplish that goal.

Raising awareness is relatively easy to do. Most people grow up thinking that the rest of the world is pretty much the same as what they know and experience. They understand that some people speak different languages, dress differently, and have different customs. Those are things that we learn from watching television and movies or browsing through a copy of *National Geographic*. Behind that superficial curtain of understanding is a world full of differences most of us have never given thought to: where do you buy food when there is no supermarket, what do you do when you are sick from malaria and the nearest doctor is a two-day journey away, or how does it feel to know that the newborn baby in your family has only a 50 percent chance of living past age five? Those are things most of us have never had to feel or deal with that are part of the everyday experience of people in the Two-Thirds world.

The key to raising awareness is in helping people understand the problem or situation. The way we do that is by breaking through the misconception that life for the rest of the world, in the things we can't see and don't think about, is much the same as it is for us. There are many ways to do this, and I have never found one method that works for everyone all the time. Some people are moved by statistics and data regarding unreached people groups or the volume of people who die from starvation every day. Others are deeply moved by films, pictures, or stories. Some others need closer exposure, as such a trip or firsthand experience of some sort.

I can remember a member of the missions committee at the church coming to me with a proposal to send a group of people to a country on a fact-finding mission. The itinerary called for a whirlwind tour of the country with brief stops at various orphanages and relief agencies. We had sponsored many trips prior to this one and all of them had been work trips—construction teams, evangelism teams, medical teams. The objectives for each of those teams had been to make a tangible contribution to the ministry of each area while becoming impacted by the culture.

I opposed the trip based upon the fact that I couldn't find anything tangible the group was going to do. I wanted our teams to build clinics and ministries. I failed to see the value of building awareness. To counter my opposition, the team leader shared his vision for what he hoped would be the long-term impact of the trip. He envisioned that out of the group he was assembling some of those people might one day give significantly, get others to give, or possibly even go to work in the area. While his vision was long-term, his strategy started with awareness. It wasn't hard to see his point. He had been part of an earlier trip to this same country where his life had been touched by the people and a small mission work there. The seed of awareness that was sown on his initial trip had blossomed into a serious commitment that had transformed his life purpose. He knew that involvement and great commitments all start with a little awareness.

The second step in the process is one of integration, where the new information begins to mix with the old information to the point that old values are exchanged for new values.

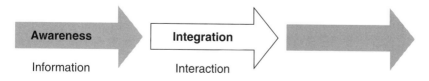

This part of the process involves interaction. Sometimes that interaction is interpersonal and sometimes cross-cultural. At other times it is an internal process that persons go through on their own. Some individuals readily embrace growth and change and look for new challenges in their own growth. Others reach a point of metamorphosis where they realize they have outgrown their old paradigms and answers. Oftentimes the interaction comes in spontaneous, unexpected ways—God's divine appointments and pop quizzes that often force us to reorder our world.

I spent all of my summers during college and graduate school working at Christian camps. One of the students who came to work with us one summer was a student from Nigeria. He was assigned to work as a kitchen helper in the main kitchen that prepared and served food for almost a thousand people every day. One morning I was rushing through the kitchen on my way to something I'm sure I thought was important when I saw this man standing alone in the food preparation room. I stopped to say hello and as I approached him I could see that he was standing next to a trash can with a tray of muffins. One by one he would pick up a muffin and throw it in the trash can. The sight wasn't all that strange to me. Every week there was food left over that was too old to be served and that the health department required us to discard after a certain number of days. What was strange was the method. Most of the kitchen helpers would just pick up the large baking sheet and slide or dump the muffins into the trash. But this man was throwing them in one at a time.

"Hi. Is everything okay?" I asked.

"You people are so fortunate and have so much. One of these muffins would keep a child in my country alive for a week."

That interaction had more of an impact on me than a truckload of pictures or the most moving message on hunger. It forced me to look at my culture, my viewpoints, and my behaviors. It's also one of the first times I can remember being humbled and ashamed at being a middle-class North American college kid. Up until then, hunger and starvation had been theoretical but now it was real because it had a face and a name and a voice.

In the integration step we look beyond the mere problem and begin to look at possible causes and potential solutions. Our interest level goes up several notches. We now begin to look for information and begin asking questions. It's also a point where we begin to abandon some of our bias and prejudice. Our behavior may not have changed radically but our investment level has increased and the problem or issue has taken on a personal nature.

The third step in the process is one of accountability. This is where true transformation takes place as people begin to change their behavior and reorder their values and change their lives.

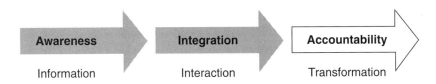

It is in the accountability stage that we look even deeper into the problem and its causes and examine our own role in creating or allowing the problem and in contributing to its solution. We have ceased to be a bystander and have reached a point where we must take initiative and begin to act.

A group of college students were genuinely moved by the theme of a college winter conference we attended on "Impacting Your World." They did not want to duplicate their other camp experiences of the past where they would get excited, get home, and get over it. Before they left the camp they banded together and agreed to meet every week to pray and explore the possibility of doing something that would make an impact. At that point they didn't know exactly what they were going to do; they just believed that there was something out there for them to do. They explored several options, did research, and ultimately decided to start a program to feed homeless people on the streets of the inner city. They discovered that there was one night of the week when none of the other agencies were providing food, so they organized and put together a program. The students either bought the food or got it donated and made all the arrangements themselves. One night a week they would show up, make the food, and go out and give it away. In the process of feeding people they developed relationships, shared their faith, and impacted a lot of people's lives.

The best part of the program was that it was all done by the students. In the two years they ran the program while I was college pastor, I went twice at their invitation to see what they were doing. To me they will always be a great example of the process we've talked about. Their awareness was raised as they received information about the abundance of needs and opportunities. They integrated the information through a process of interacting with each other and with the needs they felt they could do something about. They then ultimately brought it to a point of action as their desires, priorities, and behaviors were changed.

There are many degrees of activity and commitment that go along with accountability. Some people will create, organize, and launch into things while others are more comfortable with a smaller step of joining others as part of a team or participating in a program. It is important that we offer and support options that are attainable and within the reach of those people who are ready to act with accountability. A person may not be ready or able to change his or her career and become a missionary to the Sudan. Someone may, however, be ready to devote two weeks on a special project or commit to spending a weekend a month at an orphanage or other outreach. The rule of thumb is "If they can't take a big step, offer a smaller step; if they're not ready for a small step, offer them a baby step."

What follows is a list and description of ideas for things you can do to raise awareness, promote integration, and encourage accountability. Before we get into the lists I want to emphasize the importance of each step in the process. In the same way that I once erred in only raising awareness, I now don't want only to try to create accountability. The process takes time, and each person is on his or her own schedule. Some people move quickly to accountability and others are quite content to simply learn more about what they already seem to know. There is danger in both. The person who moves to act too quickly without fully understanding the issues can be as frustrating as the person who knows everything but does little. The important part seems to be in knowing where people are and giving them something to move toward—at whatever pace they can handle.

## Awareness Activities

Planning awareness activities is much like planning curriculum for a teacher. You first need to assess the competency level of your audience and determine what you would like them to know. That will give you some idea of the gaps in their knowledge or awareness and you design programs or activities that will fill in the gaps. It's important that we find the balance between stretching our audience and being realistic. I may want my group to be fully informed as to the current state of the unreached peoples project but that may be outside the scope of what's realistic for many of them.

One of the simplest and best ways to raise awareness is through the use of a guest speaker. It's also one of the most risky and often most misused. In my work as a consultant I never go into work with a company without first understanding the environment of the company and the desired outcomes of my client. To do so would be risky, unwise, and irresponsible. We need to adopt the same strategy when selecting a speaker and then share that information with them well in advance. Speakers should be partners with you in working toward a clear objective that you have thought out and planned in advance. It's the host's responsibility to plan how to best utilize the speaker.

One of the best speakers I have ever partnered with in this way is Pastor Von Trutzschler from Spectrum Ministries in San Diego. I have had "Von" speak to all different types of groups on various subjects regarding missions, and he has always been sensitive to my strategies and concerns. Whether it was a testosterone-driven group of high-school-age guys or a group of couples and families, he focused his presentation on the specific goal.

Good resources for speakers are reputable missions organizations, but be sure that you communicate your objectives and your audience when inquiring about speakers. Ask about their speaking experience and get a tape. If possible, go and hear them speak to another group. That will give you the best idea of how they will work with your group.

Other good awareness activities are films or videos. Many missions organizations have produced some good films. Make sure that you watch the film in advance and determine how to best utilize the film as part of your overall presentation. Don't rely on the film to have a specific closing or application for your group. Don't feel that you have to use all of a film when only certain segments speak to the issues you are interested in.

Another option is using special presentations that are offered by groups or organizations. World Vision, Compassion, or U.S. Center for World Missions often have special programs designed to tell people about what they do. Keep in mind that their objective might be slightly different from your objective. They may want to let people know about their organization or even solicit donations or responses. Regardless of how you feel about their pitch, they should also be willing to work with you on accomplishing your objective: to share information and raise the awareness of your audience.

At one church we held a special missions dinner every other month for the purpose of raising awareness. The dinners were usually themed around a certain country or part of the world. The dinners were open to everyone in the church, and each table was hosted by a member of the missions committee. We were able to do the dinner with no reservations and paid for the food by asking for donations, but that may not work in every case. Each dinner featured a presentation by either a missionary or a special missions group from the church such as our orphanage ministry or inner-city ministry. It was a nice way for people to get new information and to see what was going on in and through the church.

## Integration Activities

The purpose of integration activities is to allow people to interact with each other and with the information they possess. The action group of college students that formed out of the college conference is a simple example of an integration activity. We would regularly form these action groups whenever a group of people wanted to do something in a particular area. Many people expect the church to initiate and sponsor all programs. It's not always possible to do that, so we would set up an action group with a sponsor from the missions committee who was responsible to guide, advise, and coach the group in its process. Sometimes the groups resulted in new programs and other times they fizzled out. Either way it was due to their ownership and initiative and the process of interaction.

One of the most powerful interaction activities is the use of simulation. It's physically impossible to provide every person in the church with a face-to-face encounter with a starving person from Haiti or a lost person from Indonesia. You can, however, simulate the situations so that the people in your group are forced to interact with the issues in a powerful way. Let me show you one way we did this at camp.

As part of our summer camp theme of learning what it meant to be a "global Christian" we wanted to do something that would help students come to grips with the problem of world hunger. We decided to devote an entire day to exposing students to the problem, both intellectually and experientially. The intellectual part was fairly straightforward. We gathered resources and gave a short presentation followed by a film from World Vision. The intent was to give students an idea of the scope and the severity of the problem without jerking their emotions around. At the end of the film, we simply asked students to be willing to spend the day "walking in the feet of hungry persons." For them that meant voluntarily foregoing the best lunch of the week and staying away from the snack bar. We also told them that our dinner that evening would be a special dinner, and they would get the most out of the dinner by coming to the meal hungry.

There was a flood of questions from those people who hated not knowing what to expect. The guys wanted to know what they could look forward to eating and girls wanted to know what to wear to a world dinner. All questions were simply answered with the same response: "Trust us, you'll get more out of the dinner by coming to the meal hungry."

The first session of camp we watched eagerly because we, also, didn't know what we could expect from the students. Would any of them volunteer to skip lunch? Was there any chance they'd remember what today was about for more than thirty seconds? In spite of my years of experience in working with kids, I forget at times that they switch gears much faster than adults. They also have an amazing ability to look on the outside as if nothing is going on inside when under the surface amazing things are happening. That was the case on this day. Of the 200 students 140 skipped lunch that day.

As students came into the dining hall that evening they were given a colored ticket. Ten percent of the group were given a black ticket, 60 percent were given a yellow ticket, and 30 percent were given a red ticket. The dining hall had been set up accordingly. There were tables with linen tablecloths for the 10 percent with black tickets. There were tables with basic plates and bowls for those with the yellow tickets and no tables and no chairs for those with a red ticket. Upon entering they were instructed to go to their corresponding tables. Before the meal began they were given simple instructions: You are free to interact with anyone in any way you choose but you cannot steal food and you cannot leave the dining room.

When the food was served, the 10 percent received a full five-course meal. The 60 percent received a bowl of simple broth, a small piece of bread, and a small glass of water. The 30 percent received nothing. After all of the food had been delivered to the tables, the interactions started.

Some of those at the banquet tables readily shared their food while others hoarded it. Some shared their food until they realized they couldn't get more and then they stopped sharing. Those with the soup and bread tended to share more freely even though they had far less to share. The behaviors were fairly predictable but what was surprising were the comments from students:

> "You can't do this to me. I paid money to be here and I deserve to eat!"
> "This isn't fair. Just because other people don't have enough to eat doesn't mean I should have to be hungry."
> "Okay, I get the point. Now when can I eat?"
> "I suppose if you wanted us to know about cancer you'd give us all cancer so we'd know what it felt like."

The students were allowed to interact for twenty or twenty-five minutes. By that time the food was gone and the behaviors had been played out. Students were told that the world dinner experience typified the distribution of food in the world where 10 percent had all they could eat, 60 percent had very little, and 30 percent had nothing. They were then dismissed to discussion groups where they would have a chance to talk about their experience and what it meant to them.

This was the greatest surprise of all. Once the anger subsided and the jokes about ordering pizza stopped, the students got into some sincere discussion. They talked about their reactions and their feelings. They also talked about how they now understood hunger from a different point of view. We had allowed forty-five minutes for discussion but most groups wanted more. At the end of the discussion we invited them back into the dining hall for a small meal that we would eat together "thankfully." We felt that we needed to do this at camp because the students had paid for food and had no other means to get it. Many students, however, chose not to eat the second meal. The money the camp saved from meals forfeited by students was given to World Vision for a hunger relief project.

I have also conducted world dinners at churches as part of a world awareness day. The following is a typical outline for such a day.

| 8:30–9:00 | Registration and sign-ups |
| 9:00–10:30 | Awareness program |
| 10:30 | Break (water only) |
| 10:45–12:00 | Simulation 1 |
| 12:00 | Prayer and fasting for the world's hungry |
| 1:00 | World crafts or fundraiser preparation |
| 2:30 | Break (water only) |
| 2:45 | Program 2 |
| 4:30 | World dinner |

## Registration

In the pre-event materials, people should be told that lunch and dinner will be part of the event. They should also be told to plan to stay throughout the entire day. This is important in order for them to get the most out of the day. At registration and sign-ups you should have something to drink, such as watered-down Tang, coffee, and tea. Food is optional. You don't want to take away from the lunch or dinner experience, and you don't want to overdo it either by providing an unlimited amount of donuts or pastries. If you provide food it should be simple but appealing.

## Awareness Program

The first program should focus on informing people about the problem of world hunger. World Vision is an excellent resource for films, videos, and other information you might need. They can also furnish you with current data on the issue. You might want to focus on more than just the issue of food and include water, disease, education, health care, transportation, wars, and natural disasters. Many people fail to realize that the world hunger issue is more than just a problem of food distribution. At the end of the program, people should have the impression that world hunger is a serious problem but one that is solvable.

## Simulation

Here is a model for a simulation you might conduct as part of your world awareness day. It will give you a basis for creating your own customized version that will work with your group.

The group is divided into three equal groups: the Super Nations, the Emerging Nations, and Third-World Nations. Within each group there should be several smaller groups so that you might have three small groups of six people that make up the Super Nations. The same is true for the other two categories. Each group is given a set of cards that corresponds to their status:

| DESIGNATION | | INFLUENCE | WEALTH | PEOPLE | FOOD |
|---|---|---|---|---|---|
| Super Nations | A | 6 tickets per | 6 tickets | 1 ticket | 6 tickets |
| | B | group | per group | per | per |
| | C | | | group | group |
| Emerging Nations | A | 3 tickets per | 3 tickets | 3 tickets | 3 tickets |
| | B | group | per group | per | per |
| | C | | | group | group |
| Third-World | A | 1 ticket per | 1 ticket | 6 tickets | 1 ticket |
| Nations | B | group | per group | per | per |
| | C | | | group | group |

The ground rules are simple. Each group must make at least one trade every five minutes. If they do not they must sit out for five minutes while others trade. Trades must go two ways (i.e., I give something and I get something) but not all trades have to be one-to-one. Anyone can trade with anyone else with the following conditions: A Super Nation can force a trade with an Emerging Nation or a Third-World Nation but only on a one-to-one basis. An Emerging Nation can force a trade with a Third-World Nation but only on a one-to-one basis. A Third-World Nation cannot force a trade with anyone. Once the trade is agreed upon, each team must draw a card from its Wild Card stack before the cards are actually exchanged. The Wild Card stack card influences every deal. The Wild Card stack should contain the cards shown on page 205.

Additional cards and scenarios can be created as needed. You can create them around cultural conflicts or political uprisings or any number of things. Some can also have positive results such as the signing of agreements.

Each team should assign one person to be the Timekeeper, one person to be the Accountant, one person to be the keeper of the Wild Cards, and the rest as Trade Negotiators. Should anyone ask about the goal or objective, the answer is to trade among countries and redistribute the resources in whatever ways they see fit. This allows

| | |
|---|---|
| **Sanctioned Trade**<br>The Deal Goes Through<br>As Planned<br><br><br>*(Five of these cards and one<br>each of the other cards.)* | A **natural disaster** has hit your<br>country. If you are an EN or a TWN<br>you have five minutes to get a food<br>ticket from two different SNs or sit<br>out ten minutes. If you are an SN<br>you may not trade a food ticket for<br>ten minutes. |
| **War** has just broken out in<br>your country. This deal is off<br>and you cannot trade for the<br>next five minutes. | **Economic Downturn**<br>If you are an SN you must give<br>away two wealth tickets to another<br>SN or an EN. If you are an EN you<br>must give away one wealth ticket<br>to another EN or an SN. If you are<br>a TWN your next trade must be for<br>a wealth ticket. |
| **Terrorism Strikes**<br>SNs must give away two influence<br>tickets to a TWN and the TWN must<br>give two food tickets to the SN.<br>If ENs are involved, trade is one<br>influence ticket for one food ticket. | **Bad weather and poor harvest.**<br>If the trade involves any food<br>tickets the trade is off. |

them to determine the criteria whereby the resources will be redistributed. Let the simulation go for fifteen or twenty minutes until things begin to flow and trades are happening more quickly. Intervene and ask them to total up all of their tickets. If any groups now have more tickets than the groups that were previously above them on the chart, they must now switch roles. In this scenario, the three groups with the most tickets are now the Super Nations, the next three become the Emerging Nations, and the next three the Third World Nations. Before they start again tell them that trades must now be done in four minutes or less.

Leave at least twenty minutes for a debrief. Part of the debrief can be done in small groups and part can be done as a whole group. The small groups should have representatives from each of the various country groups. The debrief should be simple and follow this basic format:

What happened?
What was your role as a group? As an individual?
What did you experience? (Hear from the different groups.)
What were you feeling? What was going on inside you?
What assumptions or interpretations did you make?
What parts of the experience were easy for you?
What parts were difficult for you?
What would you do differently?
What do you think you learned?

## Prayer and Fasting Service

After the simulation tell the group that you are going to devote the lunch hour to praying and fasting for the world's hungry. You might want to review with your group what the Bible has to say about fasting and its purposes. One way to make the hour go quickly is to structure the time in the same way you would set up a concert of prayer (see David Bryant's book, *Concerts of Prayer,* IVP).

10 min.   Start with an introduction, a few Scriptures and possibly a song of praise. Pray individually for cleansing, forgiveness, and to remove anything that might be standing in the way of God speaking to you.

10 min.   Get together with one other person. Share briefly how the other person might pray for you and then pray for each other.

10 min.   Sing a song and then get into a group of four to pray specifically for your church or group. Pray for your church leaders.

10 min.   Pray for the hungry and needy close by in your city or county. Pray for their needs and for those groups that are attempting to reach them.

10 min.   Get into a group of eight to pray for the hungry and needy around the world. Use this opportunity to have people pray for specific countries they are interested in or where your church sponsors missionaries. You might want to use one of the resource books or prayer cards from the U.S. Center for World Missions.

10 min.   Gather as a whole group to pray for government and world leaders, for heads of missions organizations who sit in positions of power that they might be touched and influenced. Sing a song to close.

## World Crafts/Fundraiser Preparation

This is one way to begin to turn people toward working on part of a solution. This time can either be used to assemble crafts that represent different parts of the Third World or to sort and price items to be sold at a street fair sponsored by your church. Contact the missionaries your church sponsors well in advance and ask them for some simple craft ideas or explore the possibility of having them ship items to you that you can sell at a street fair. One church that is heavily involved in Haiti has an annual street fair at the church on Sunday mornings. At the fair people may buy Haitian dolls, artwork, or other handicrafts. They also have the opportunity to sponsor a Haitian child at a booth that has information on children needing sponsors. Preparing for such an event as part of your world awareness day is a good way to begin to get people involved.

## Program 2

This is where you want to begin to tie all of the events together and focus on what you want people to know, feel, and do after the day is over. This is not a time to give them a lot of new information but rather to help them process the information and experiences they have had already. One way to do this is by showcasing what some other groups are doing successfully. Tell some success stories and focus on what can and is being done. As part of the program you may want to break into small groups and have a discussion. The discussion should begin to bridge the gap between what they have learned and experienced and how it will change the way they live. This is a turn toward accountability, that is, "What are you going to do differently now that you've had this experience?" Remember to focus on small, achievable steps rather than the dedication of my whole life with no clear direction on what I'm supposed to do tomorrow.

At the conclusion of the program have a place they can go to get more information or a way to sign up to get involved. Some of the people will be ready to commit to an area of service. Others may need more time to process the experience. Have an option for them to join an action group or a committee where they can continue the interaction process.

## World Dinner

The world dinner can be conducted as I've described but it will have a different kind of effect and energy. People have already taken part in one simulation and they spent the day thinking about the needs of the world. Be prepared for them to be ready to share and give rather than hoard. Either way the experience is valid. It forms a graphic portrayal of the world situation and reminds of us of how blessed we are and how thankful we should be. It also reminds us that we have a responsibility to the rest of the world. Make sure you bring closure to the experience and to the day. While the problem is overwhelming, the solution still is as simple as each person doing their part to make a difference. I love World Vision's response to the question "How do you begin to feed a world full of starving people?" The answer: "One person at a time."

## Accountability Activities

There is a principle of involvement that seems to be universally valid. It is that out of any given group of people 5 percent will be innovators, 15 percent will be adapters and 80 percent will be adopters. What that means for us is that when moved to do something, 5 percent of the people will start something, 15 percent will adapt something they've seen, and 80 percent will sign up for what's already in place. When persons reach a point of accountability that doesn't necessarily mean they are going to organize a whole new ministry. Some will but most won't.

This means that in our programming we need to have options for people to get involved in and allow for the creation or adaptation of other options. In the college ministry we had a monthly trip to poor areas of Mexico, one or more short-term missions trips a year, and the Homeless Feeding Program that was started by students. The objective was to always have at least one ongoing ministry that was an easy way for people to get involved. We also wanted to have a way for people to get more involved, get more exposure, and make a greater contribution. Those were our short-term trips. We did trips to Haiti, Guatemala, Eastern Europe, France, Costa Rica, and the inner cities of Boston and Philadelphia. Many of those students later went on to do longer-term trips with other agencies or became career missionaries.

We also tried to create an environment in which people who had an idea and a burden could act on it. The Homeless Feeding Program was just one example of what some of the innovators came up with. At different times we also had a convalescent home ministry and a juvenile hall ministry. There was also a Big Brother/Big Sister program that never fully got off the ground due to unwieldy legal requirements.

In creating an environment conducive to accountability you should have the following:

One program that is within easy reach of anyone who is ready to get involved.

One program for those who are ready to take a bigger step and requires more from them.

A means of support, guidance, and coaching for those people who want to take ownership of their own ideas and create something.

The operative word is ownership. There is no accountability in ideas alone. The person or group of people must be willing to take ownership and be committed to the cause. The role of the ministry professional is to make sure they receive support, guidance, and coaching.

This raises the issue of the comfort level of the ministry professional. I spent many hours worrying about the ideas of some of these people and groups. I feared for their failure and often wanted to spare them disappointment. But I also had to look at the other side. What kind of message do I send to people if I raise their awareness, encourage them in their interaction, and then when it comes time to do something they have to let me do it? I wonder if we often spend so much time stuck in raising people's awareness because it is a relatively safe place—for them and for us.

If there is a safe place in Christian ministry it is surely not in the area of missions. What greater way for our faith to be put into action than by our involvement with the hungry, hurting, and lost of the world? For in those moments we most resemble the one whose life we seek to emulate.

It is not the critic who counts, not the one who points out how the strong man stumbled or how the doer of deeds might have done them better. The credit belongs to the one who is actually in the arena, whose face is marred with sweat and dust and blood; who strives valiantly; who errs and comes short again and again; who knows the great enthusiasms, the great devotions and spends himself in a worthy cause; who if he wins, knows the triumphs of high achievement; and who, if he fails, at least fails while daring greatly, so that his place shall never be with those cold and timid souls who know neither victory nor defeat.

Theodore Roosevelt

*Todd Alexander was college and missions pastor at South Coast Community Church in Irvine, California. He co-founded U.S. Students Against World Hunger, an organization dedicated to educating students to the problems and solutions of world hunger. He is now the principal consultant of Alexander and Associates in San Diego.*

# Notes

## Chapter 2: Igniting Volunteers to Become World Christians

1. Nelson Bell, *Foreign Devil in China* (Grand Rapids: Zondervan).
2. Dietrich Bonhoeffer, *Life Together* (New York: Harper and Row, 1954), 101.
3. Charles Swindoll, *Improving Your Serve* (Waco: Word, 1981), 52–53.

## Chapter 4: Focusing on Priorities: People versus Projects

1. Mary Fisher, "The Key to Ministry: Focus on Relationships not Programs," *The 1993 Great Commission Handbook* (Evanston, Ill.: Berry Publishing Services, 1993), 21.

## Chapter 5: Selecting and Screening Volunteers for Service

1. D. Hicks, "Trial by Team," in *Stepping Out* (Seattle: YWAM Publishing, 1992), 97.
2. C. Hawthorne, "Not Thirsty, Still Hungry," in *Stepping Out* (Seattle: YWAM Publishing, 1992), 31.
3. T. Hoke, "Follow The Leader," in *Stepping Out* (Seattle: YWAM Publishing, 1992), 101.

## Chapter 7: Cooperating with Church Leaders

1. W. H. Stewart and W. E. Yeager, "The Youth Minister and the Senior Pastor," in *The Complete Book of Youth Ministry,* ed. W. S. Benson and M. H. Senter (Chicago: Moody, 1987).
2. P. Borthwick, *Organizing Your Youth Ministry* (Grand Rapids: Zondervan, 1988), chap. 17.
3. P. Borthwick, "Youth mission trips," in *Methods for Youth Ministry,* ed. D. Roadcup (Cincinnati: Standard, 1986).
4. R. Burns, *Create in Me a Youth Ministry* (Wheaton: Victor, 1986). See "Planning a Mission Trip," p. 88.
5. Ibid.
6. Ibid.
7. Ibid.

## Chapter 8: Legal and Liability Issues

1. The issue of ransom payments is one of grave concern to mission agencies. A decision to pay ransom has implications not only for the church involved in the kidnapping, but also for other mission agencies working in the same country. There are tax and federal criminal law implications as well. Any church that is considering a policy that would allow the payment of ransom in a kidnap situation is encouraged to carefully consider the implications of that policy. If a church is not familiar with these implications it should obtain competent legal counsel to assist it with the legal issues and explore the issue further with experienced mission professionals.

## Chapter 11: Training and Preparing for the Trip

1. C. Eaton and K. Hurst, *Vacations with a Purpose* (Colorado Springs, Colo.: NavPress, 1991).

# Annotated Bibliography
# of Missions-Related Books

Aeschliman, Gordon, ed. 1992. *Short-term mission handbook: A comprehensive guide for participants and leaders.* Evanston, Ill.: Berry Publishing Services.

    A sequel to *Stepping Out,* this volume has over sixty new articles and current information on more than two hundred services, training, and resource opportunities. It covers all you need to know about planning and taking a short-term mission trip. It is a vital resource for individuals, churches, school groups, and mission organizations.

Ahonen, Lauri. 1984. *Missions growth.* Pasadena: William Carey Library.

    Many books investigate the growth of churches and church movements. This short book is the only serious study of the growth of mission structures, the specific example being the outstanding growth of the Finnish Free Foreign Mission, the common mission board for the independent Pentecostal churches of Finland.

Anderson, Neil, and Hyatt Moore. 1992. *In search of the source.* Portland: Multnomah.

    Through this compelling true story of Bible translators Neil and Carol Anderson, we relearn something we may have forgotten . . . the raw power of God's Word to wrench human lives from darkness and flood the earth with light, understanding, and peace. This is not only the gripping story of a man who brings the Bible to a stone-age culture, it is also a much bigger story of how the Scriptures pierce and transform an entire civilization.

Barnett, Betty. 1991. *Friend raising.* YWAM Publishing.

    This 178-page paperback book focuses on bringing together God's plan for biblical missions support. It includes principles proven in the mission field. The book is a strong dose of common sense, mixed with that rare spice, respect for the donor, and liberally garnished with the conviction that God supplies needs through mutually satisfying relationships. In a world overwhelmed by fund-raising hype and gimmicks, Betty Barnett presents a refreshing biblical alternative.

Barrett, David B., and Todd M. Johnson. 1990. *Our globe and how to reach it*. Eastbourne: New Hope.
A concise, comprehensive, and up-to-date picture of the push for evangelization worldwide. Using facts, diagrams, common sense and the most advanced and comprehensive missions data base available anywhere, Barrett and Johnson provide readers with an authoritative, clear, and fresh look at the global evangelization movement.

Beals, Paul. 1988. *A people for his name*. Grand Rapids: Baker.
Almost no book could be a superior guidebook for members of a local church mission committee. Delightful, comprehensive coverage of the local church as a biblical sending body, including the practical outworking of its mission responsibilities and relationship to mission agencies.

Borthwick, Paul. 1989. *A mind for missions*. Colorado Springs: NavPress.
A paperback that addresses the biblical mandate of going to the mission field. There are ten chapters dealing primarily with issues related to going to the missions field (e.g., the Scriptures, current events in the world, prayer, reading materials as preparation, fellowship, giving). It is directed toward college courses in missions.

———. 1988. *Youth and missions*. Wheaton: Victor.
This book is directed primarily at helping youth pastors expand the world view of young people. Unit headings emphasize expanding a student's world view by example, exposure, experiences, and through results. It is focused toward helping young people become aware of world mission-related issues.

Bryant, David. 1984. *In the gap: Become a world Christian and stand in the gap*. Ventura: Regal.
This core handbook describes what a world Christian is, how he or she thinks, what he or she chooses, and how he or she takes action for Christ's global cause.

Burnett, David. 1988. *Unearthly powers*. Eastbourne: MARC.
Primal religions pervade every nation: for some they are the foundations of life, for others their influence is unrecognized but crucial. This book deals with ghosts, possession, the evil eye, and sorcery in touch with the lives of many people. This is an especially good book, because all missionaries need to be aware of the spiritual powers and struggles that exist in primal societies.

Burns, Ridge, and Noel Bechetti. 1990. *The complete student missions handbook*. Grand Rapids: Zondervan.
A practical guide for junior- and senior-high pastors to mobilize their youth for mission projects. This book is filled with worksheets and forms for the youth

worker to use. It is written specifically for the youth minister. It comes across as childish but has excellent material.

Caldwell, Larry W. 1992. *Sent out!* Pasadena: William Carey Library.

    Because many Christians do not know what to do with the spiritual gifts of the apostle, Larry Caldwell attempts to shed new light on the confusion. He carefully analyzes the biblical evidence anew from the perspectives of both theology and missiology. Caldwell concludes that apostleship is a legitimate spiritual gift for the mission of the church today, especially for those who are pioneer missionaries planting churches in cross-cultural situations.

Chao, Jonathan. 1988. *Wise as serpents, harmless as doves.* Pasadena: William Carey Library.

    What do the Christians in China really say? From peasants to professors, from the pre-Cultural Revolution era to the present day, Chinese Christians have truly learned to act "wise as serpents, harmless as doves." In their own voices, Christians speak of the difficulty of walking the delicate line between compliance with the authorities and obedience to our Lord.

Coleman, Robert E. 1992. *The great commission lifestyle.* Grand Rapids: Baker.

    When it comes to obeying Jesus Christ's command to disciple all nations, are you a bit uncertain how to begin? In this book, Coleman shows how discipleship is designed to be a way of life for all Christians. A study guide is included to make the book useful for both individuals and groups.

Collins, Marjorie A. 1986. *Manual for today's missionary: From recruitment to retirement.* Pasadena: William Carey Library.

    In down-to-earth style Marjorie Collins covers the areas of preparation, field experience, furlough, and retirement. Not just an essential handbook for missionaries, this is an invaluable text for missions courses, an orientation tool for mission boards, and an excellent reference guide for pastors, youth workers, libraries, for all who are interested in missions and missionaries.

————. 1974. *Who cares about the missionary?* Chicago: Moody.

    This thoroughly practical book lists numerous ways and means by which Christians can more fully cooperate in the response to the Great Commission to "go into all the world and preach the gospel." The suggestions range from how to pray and mission awareness to personal involvement and short-term missions. It is a great book for churches to understand the importance of supporting and sending missionaries.

Danker, William. 1971. *Profit for the Lord.* Grand Rapids: Eerdmans.

    A surprising account of the various ways in which missionaries have utilized business enterprises to assist the planting of the church and to benefit new converts. It specifically studies the Moravians and the Basel Mission Trading Company, concentrating on the economic structures they created to support their mission work.

Dawson, John. 1989. *Taking our cities for God.* Altamonte Springs, Fla.: Creation House.

This is a highly readable, moving, passionate book. Not a technical study of urban missions, it is no armchair treatment either. It is highly informed, the work of the leader of one of the largest urban outreaches, as well as being a profound inspiration. It teaches how to break spiritual strongholds in order to win people for Christ.

Dick, Lois Hoadley. 1987. *Isobel Kuhn.* Minneapolis: Bethany House.

After reading about Hudson Taylor and the China Inland Mission, Isobel Miller felt a call to China and, specifically, to the Lisu people. In China she married John Kuhn and together they faced hardships, long separations, severe illness, war, and death. Yet through all this the church among the Lisu people grew in faith and the knowledge of Jesus Christ. A challenging and inspiring story which gives new understanding to "pioneer missionary work."

Duewel, Wesley. 1990. *Mighty prevailing prayer.* Grand Rapids: Zondervan.

One of the best books on teaching how to prevail in prayer to come off the press in a century. A must for every serious Christian. God has a more effective prayer life for all Christians, especially for pastors and missionaries; this book is a guide.

———. 1986. *Touch the world through prayer.* Grand Rapids: Zondervan.

A remarkable book by a truly remarkable mission statesman who is widely known as a man of prayer. But it also compellingly explains how every Christian can pray for missionaries, church leaders, and political leaders in countries around the globe where the gospel is being preached today. Includes specific Bible promises that we can claim in these intercessory prayers.

Eaton, Chris, and Kim Hurst. 1991. *Vacations with a purpose.* Colorado Springs: NavPress.

This brief book helps first-time short-termers understand what they need to know before going to the mission field. It includes a section for journal reflections while on the trip and a debriefing section for reflecting on the experience. Brief and sketchy in places.

Echerd, Pam, and Alice Arathoon, eds. 1989. *Understanding and nurturing the missionary family.* Pasadena: William Carey Library.

Compendium of the International Conference on Missionary Kids, Quito, Ecuador, 1987, Volume 1. Forty key presentations at the International Conference on Missionary Kids. The best there is on the most crucial subject in missions today.

———, ed. 1989. *Planning for MK nurture.* Pasadena: William Carey Library.

Compendium of the International Conference on Missionary Kids, Quito, Ecuador, 1987, Volume 2. The most thorough, professional treatment by the whole group of experts of the complex task of raising kids on the mission field.

Elliston, Edgar J. 1993. *Home grown leaders.* Pasadena: William Carey Library.

This book aims at providing an approach for the development of Christian leaders, whether they be small-group leaders, supervisors of multiple small groups, or pastors. It relies on both a biblical foundation and contemporary leadership theory. The book is currently being used to inform leadership trainers at several levels in different parts of the world.

Filbeck, David. 1985. *Social context and proclamation.* Pasadena: William Carey Library.

Few contributions to the understanding of communication, especially cross-culturally, have been done from several fields of inquiry: sociology, anthropology, linguistics, and missiology. This unique, integrative approach breathes the intimate knowledge of an active missionary, as well as a highly competent group of the technical factors.

Foyle, Marjory F. 1988. *Overcoming missionary stress.* Wheaton: Evangelical Missions Information Services.

Stress is a natural part of a healthy life. But too much stress can damage relationships, hamper productivity, even ruin lives. Living in alien, often hostile cultures, typically without support networks, missionaries are especially vulnerable to stress. This book deals with stress in all forms: missionary marriage, singleness, relationships with co-workers, raising children, culture shock, handling burnout, and mental health.

Gallagher, Neil. 1977. *Don't go overseas until you've read this book.* Minneapolis: Bethany Fellowship.

This book gives prospective missionaries a helpful preview of what is ahead and will help steer them clear of pitfalls. Topics that are discussed are culture shock, misunderstanding, and persecution. This book is not just for missionaries; it is also for tourists, students, and businessmen.

Garrison, V. David. 1990. *The nonresidential missionary.* Eastbourne: MARC/New Hope.

The nonresidential missionary is a career foreign missionary who is matched up with a single unevangelized population segment, but who lives somewhere other than in their midst because legal residence for a missionary is prohibited or highly restricted. These missionaries survey the situation of the population group, become fluent in the language, and mobilize every form of Christian ministry to the group. They concentrate on the initial evangelization and on eliminating gaps or duplications with other mission agencies.

Greenway, Roger S., and Timothy M. Monsma. 1989. *Cities: Missions' new frontier.* Grand Rapids: Baker.

Students of missions will need to wrestle with urban issues if they are to be prepared for ministry in tomorrow's world. Chapters include opportunities to reach "all peoples" provided by current immigration patterns in North America,

the challenges of burgeoning Third-World cities, effective methods of spreading
the gospel, and ameliorating urban social problems.

Grunlan, Stephen, and Marvin K. Mayer. 1988. *Cultural anthropology: A Christian
perspective.* Grand Rapids: Zondervan.
    This book is an interesting gateway to the complex field of cultural anthro-
pology. It may be studied with profit by anyone whose sphere of activity includes cross-cultural communication. As the title states, this book is a Christian
approach to all aspects of anthropology. This is a very helpful book for missionaries as well as urban evangelists.

Hamilton, Donald. 1987. *Tentmakers speak.* TMQ Research.
    This book provides you with the invaluable insight of over four hundred vet-
eran tentmakers worldwide. There is no better way to see the tentmaking potential for both missionaries under standard agencies and those who are working by themselves.

Hampton, Vanita, and Carol Plueddemann. 1991. *World shapers.* Wheaton: Harold
Shaw.
    Throughout the years, the voices and writings of great missionaries have in-
spired future generations with the cause of global missions. Now the poignant
and powerful quotes from many of these heroes of the faith are organized in a
treasury for inspiration and reflection. Quotes by William Carey, Amy Car-
michael, Robert Moffat, Mary Slessor, Hudson and Maria Taylor, Eric Lidell, Jim
Elliot, and many others. Ideal as a source of quotes for prayer and newsletters,
or for personal challenge.

Hedlund, Roger E. 1991. *The mission of the church in the world.* Grand Rapids: Baker.
    A missionary to India presents a fresh, Asian perspective on what the work
of the church is about. This is a book about the Bible and missions written from
the standpoint of Christians standing toe-to-toe with followers of other faiths.
Its solid biblical exegesis, unquestionable evangelical stance, and magnificent
obsession to reach the unreached makes this book a must for the missionary
thinkers.

Hesselgrave, David J. 1980. *Planting churches cross-culturally.* Grand Rapids: Baker.
    This is a practical and biblical book offering serious students and practition-
ers of mission a step-by-step approach to developing a master plan for entering
a new community with a church-planting program. Each aspect of the master
plan is developed theologically, scientifically, and practically. Cultural differences are analyzed, and missionaries are guided in how to transcend their own
cultural background.

―――. 1988. *Today's choices for tomorrow's mission.* Grand Rapids: Zondervan.
    This book offers a wide-ranging, in-depth discussion of critical issues facing
mission leaders and strategists. Based on significant research, the material is
compelling and thought-provoking. It plows right into sensitive topics, and

gives fair hearing to those who differ. It has a marvelous grip on the basic questions in the cause of missions today.

Hiebert, Paul G. 1985. *Anthropological insight for missionaries.* Grand Rapids: Baker.
In order for the missionaries to be successful, they must understand the people they serve in their historical and original settings. They must understand themselves similarly. Otherwise, the missionaries' works may be without meaning and relevance. This book explores the anthropological aspect of mission, so that men and women of God may apply themselves more effectively in a different cultural setting.

Hodges, Melvin. 1976. *The indigenous church.* Springfield: Gospel Publishing House.
A classic. Few books have had the global impact of this one. Examines the New Testament church and the biblical basis of missions in the Book of Acts. Building on the Bible, it explores minutely the methods of starting truly indigenous churches on the mission field.

————. 1978. *The indigenous church and the missionary.* Pasadena: William Carey Library.
One of the most famous missionary church planters of all time, Hodges now turns his attention to the unique pressures, problems, and opportunities the new national churches present to the expatriate missionaries still on the scene. This slim little pocket-sized book is about the most valuable book any missionary can own and often consult.

Hofman, J. Samuel. 1993. *Mission work in today's world.* Pasadena: William Carey Library.
This helpful and practical book contains short and easy-to-read articles written out of the author's experiences as a missionary in Chiapas, Mexico. Topics covered are the missionary's first years; leadership training at home and abroad; opposition, persecution, and competition; response to the political scene; mission theory and practices; and coming back to the church at home.

Jacobs, Donald. 1991. *From rubble to rejoicing.* Pasadena: William Carey Library.
God used Nehemiah to lead the people to rebuild Jerusalem, from rubble to rejoicing. The Spirit-given principles of leadership are seen clearly in the Book of Nehemiah, and this book will lead you in a study of those principles that are vital in missions.

Jabbour, Nabeel. 1993. *Rumbling volcano.* Pasadena: Mandate, William Carey Library.
One of the few books written by someone who is as close to being an insider as is possible without actually being a Muslim. Possibly the first text written in which Islamic fundamentalism is objectively and compassionately examined (and not attacked). The author shows what it is like to understand the leaders

in the movement such as Khumeini, Hasannal Banna, Sayyid Qutb, and others, and attempts to understand Islamic fundamentalism from the inside.

Johnstone, Patrick. 1986. *Operation world.* Pasadena: William Carey Library.
    Prayer changes things! This book is a unique resource for Christians who want God to use their prayers to change the world. It has listings of different countries and information about them. It is a good study resource in preparation for missions; also a prayer guide for those who want to pray for the missionaries and Christians of that particular nation.

Kauwling, Lara Jean, ed. 1990. *Lifetime memories annual: Summer missions handbook 1991.* La Mirada: Biola University Student Missionary Union.
    This book is designed to aid those who are interested in summer missions opportunity. It is a collection of over one hundred different mission organizations that have ministries available for anyone who is interested in short-term mission. The first three chapters help prepare passports, visas, and other paperwork; the rest of the book is the listings of different organizations.

Kane, J. Herbert. 1989. *A concise history of the Christian world mission.* Grand Rapids: Baker.
    This book is an excellent introductory survey of Christian missions from A.D. 30 to the twentieth century. Dr. Kane emphasizes the importance of all believers to have a working knowledge of the Christian world mission. It is a highly effective tool for adult Bible study or mission training in a local church.

————. 1985. *A global view of Christian missions: From Pentecost to the present.* Grand Rapids: Baker.
    This book is a comprehensive survey of the progress of Christian mission effort from Pentecost to the present. The book is divided into two parts. Part 1 discusses the development of Christianity and its mission from the Roman Empire into North America. Part 2 is comprised of country-by-country reports including political history, efforts, and results. It is profitable and enjoyable reading for students and laymen alike.

————. 1985. *Christian missions in biblical perspective.* Grand Rapids: Baker.
    This book is divided into five parts: the biblical basis of missions; the trinitarian dimension of mission; the theological imperatives of mission; the historical context of missions; and the spiritual dynamics of missions. Dr. Kane unashamedly adheres to a high view of the Scriptures and emphasizes that the Bible is the reliable, authentic, and authoritative Word of God; that the church is still the salt of the earth and the light of the world.

————. 1986. *Wanted: World Christian.* Grand Rapids: Baker.
    In this book Herbert Kane challenges American Christians with the fact that the prime function of the church between Pentecost and the second coming is witness not worship, evangelism not exhortation. The responsibility for world-

wide witnesses rests not on a chosen few, but on the Christian community as a whole.

Keysser, Christian. 1980. *A people reborn.* Pasadena: William Carey Library.
Nothing like this exists in any other book: how does a whole tribe become Christian? Can a group be born again? Here is the high drama of a provocative mission strategy unfolded in a river valley, told by a brilliant and intrepid German missionary. This is the remarkable story of the transformation of a vigorous tribal people in New Guinea into a sound church. Brings together anthropology and biblical theology. Shows the doctrines of church, ministry and discipline working together.

Kim, Young Yun. 1988. *Communication and cross-cultural adaptation.* Philadelphia: Multilingual Matters.
Cross-cultural adaptation of immigrants, refugees, and sojourners has been extensively investigated in the social sciences, but without an integrative theoretical foundation necessary for comprehensive understanding. This book attempts to meet this need by presenting an interdisciplinary, multidimensional theory, synthesizing the existing conceptualizations and empirical evidence in anthropology, communication, psychiatry, psychology, sociology, sociolinguistics, and related disciplines into a single theoretical scheme.

Kinsler, F. Ross, and James H. Emery, eds. 1992. *Opting for change.* Pasadena: William Carey Library.
Theological Education by Extension (TEE) is often portrayed as a vision and a movement for the renewal of ministry in the church and in the world. The task of evaluation is to translate that vision into concepts and criteria that can be applied to the various components of TEE programs. This handbook is concerned primarily with self-evaluation in relation to planning, that is, ways in which people who are engaged in TEE can clarify their goals and assess results in order to pursue those goals more effectively.

Kraakevik, James H., and Dotsey Welliver, eds. 1992. *Partners in the gospel.* Wheaton: Billy Graham Center.
At the Working Consultation on Partnership in World Mission, mission executives and prominent evangelical leaders explored the increasingly important role of partnership in world evangelization. Groups interested in establishing partnerships, as well as believers pursuing greater unity in the body of Christ, will find valuable help in this book.

Kraft, Charles H. 1991. *Communication theory for Christian witness.* Maryknoll, N.Y.: Orbis.
This book draws upon faith experience and the social sciences to make pastors, preachers, missionaries, and religious educators aware of the mystery of human communication in the service of the God who calls all into communion. The question is how to communicate with those of other cultures so that the message is effectively transmitted and received. How do we recognize the

gaps—of language, tradition, experience—that separate us, and build bridges over them?

Kyle, John. 1987. *Finishing the task.* Ventura: Regal Books/Gospel Light.
    Meeting at the exact historic site of the 1806 Haystack Prayer Meeting, a number of key leaders present challenging addresses on the occasion of the 175th anniversary of a significant new beginning in world missions. But this time they talk about finishing the task.

Lewis, Jonathan. 1987. *World mission.* Pasadena: William Carey Library.
    A three-volume manual for group or individual study. Volume 1: *The Biblical/Historical Foundation;* volume 2: *The Strategic Dimension;* volume 3: *Cross-Cultural Considerations.*

Lewis, Jonathan, and Dawn Lewis. 1990. *World mission leader's guide.* Pasadena: William Carey Library.
    This guidebook is designed for the leader of a small study group using the *World Mission* manuals (vols. 1–3) in a church or a small group context.

Lewis, Norm. 1990. *Priority one: What God wants.* Pasadena: William Carey Library.
    Clearly, forcefully, and biblically articulates the Christian's marching orders. Christians who are committed to the goals of the church will help it recapture its original role to take the gospel to everyone and make disciples of all nations.

Lingenfelter, Sherwood. 1992. *Transforming culture.* Grand Rapids: Baker.
    Cross-cultural evangelists historically have attempted to transplant Western church culture in their work with other peoples. The author maintains that Western-style churches often remain irrelevant, and indigenization brings deadly compromise. The book proposes that the more biblical focus is to enable the new believers to understand the inevitable conflict between social environment and Christ. Lingenfelter reveals how subtle but pervasive cultural differences can cause conflict in churches and offers insight into how to unify a congregation with diverse cultural values.

Lingenfelter, Sherwood G., and Marvin K. Mayers. 1986. *Ministering cross-culturally.* Grand Rapids: Baker.
    When a missionary and a pastor minister to people from different cultural and social backgrounds, they invariable experience tension and conflict. To reduce this tension and improve the quality of their ministries, they need to learn about interpersonal relationships. This book is especially helpful because it provides a theoretical base for improving relationships between people of different cultures. There are numerous illustrations drawn from the authors' experiences and much of its contents are drawn from the Bible.

Livingstone, Greg. 1993. *Planting churches in Muslim cities.* Grand Rapids: Baker.
    Building on the example of more than one hundred missionaries, Livingstone's own diverse experience in missions, the Acts model, and church-growth

theory, the author teaches missionaries to help Christians in Islamic communities "think church."

Lum, Ada. 1984. *A hitchhiker's guide to missions*. Downers Grove, Ill.: InterVarsity.
 With wit and wisdom, Lum focuses on who missionaries should be, and what they should and shouldn't do. Along the way she discusses how to make disciples across cultures, how to get along with your boss and co-workers, how to deal with singleness, and how to move on to a new ministry. This book challenges and encourages all who would consider God's call anywhere.

McQuilkin, Robertson. 1984. *The great omission: A biblical basis for world evangelism*. Grand Rapids: Baker.
 A prominent mission statesman focuses perceptively on the mystery of why so many Christians, who say they have accepted Christ, refuse to accept his Great Commission! A clear-eyed, hard-hitting exposure of a crucial question.

Nida, Eugene A. 1990. *Message and mission: The communication of the Christian faith*. Pasadena: William Carey Library.
 This book uniquely equips the readers to best communicate Christianity to people of diverse backgrounds through the study of means and methods. It is a helpful book for all who are planning on mission work. In order to be effective messengers, we must first understand the dynamics, symbols, cultures, forms, meanings, religions, and techniques of other cultures.

O'Donnell, Kelly S., ed. 1992. *Missionary care*. Pasadena: William Carey Library.
 One of the pressing issues facing the missions community today is the care of its people. Evangelizing the unreached is not without its costs. Missionaries thus need and deserve the best care possible to keep them resilient and effective. This book, a handbook for supporting and developing missionary personnel, is a collaborative effort of over twenty authors to address some of the cutting edges of missionary care.

O'Donnell, Kelly S., and Michele Lewis O'Donnell. 1988. *Helping missionaries grow: Readings in mental health and missions*. Pasadena: William Carey Library.
 This book is divided into four parts: missionary preparation (candidate selection, psychological assessment, effectiveness, training); missionary families (family life, missionary couples, children, education); missionary adjustment (entering new culture, stress, relationship, attrition); special issues (agencies, women in missions, repatriation, cross-cultural counseling). These are all important issues concerning missions preparation.

Ohrt, Wallace. 1990. *The accidental missionaries*. Downers Grove, Ill.: InterVarsity.
 This book is a story about two missionaries named Denny and Jeanne Grindall. They have no formal university, seminary, or missionary training. Yet their ministry was effective and powerful, because like the first-century Christians, they knew how to love people as friends, not as objects of charity. They are one of our greatest role models as missionaries and students.

Olson, Bruce E. 1993. *Bruchko.* Altemonte Springs, Fla.: Creation House.
    Almost no single missionary story is more unbelievable and yet incredibly true: a naive nineteen-year-old, captured by stone-age Indians, gained their confidence and won them to Christ. The story continues today, as this edition will explain.

Palmer, Donald C. 1991. *Managing conflict creatively.* Pasadena: William Carey Library.
    A practical, Bible-centered approach to the dynamics of conflict and styles of conflict management. This manual is intended to serve as a teaching and study guide for a series of five seminar sessions or as a study guide for a course on conflict management in Bible institutes or seminaries. It is a guide intended for missionaries and Christian workers.

Patterson, George. 1989. *Perspective ministry career guide.* Institute of International Studies.
    A collection of workbooks to help a serious world Christian, with the help of a mentor, to take steps of learning and obedience. Helps keep a person on track through the process of discerning most fruitful avenues of cross-cultural missions ministry.

Pettifer, Julian, and Richard Bradley. 1990. *Missionaries.* London: BBC Books.
    Much of the material for this book was gathered during the making of the BBC television series *Missionaries.* The aim of the program was to take a long, close look at a largely forgotten band of men and women. Only sensational stories of missionaries disgraced, expelled, kidnapped, or murdered attract the attention of the secular press and media. This book is especially helpful, because it shows us the real heroes and saints of our culture.

Pierce, Robert Willard. 1964. *Emphasizing missions in the local church.* Grand Rapids: Zondervan.
    This book contains pages of thrilling new ideas guaranteed to boost missions in every department of your church. It is a handy work guide for pastors and church workers, prepared as a ministry of missionary challenge.

Pirolo, Neal. 1991. *Serving as senders: Six ways to support your missionaries.* Long Beach: Emmaus Road.
    This key book makes the strategic point that mobilizers, the senders, are as crucial to the cause of missions as the front-line missionaries. It is a book crammed with solid, exciting insights on the most hurting link in today's mission movement.

Poynor, Alice. 1986. *From the campus to the world.* Downers Grove, Ill.: Inter-Varsity.
    The Great Commission has always been fueled by young people with a vision for the whole world. It is no surprise then that Student Foreign Missions Fellowship (SFMF) has played a vital role in the lives of hundreds who have spread

around the globe with the good news of Christ. This book is a collection of stories of the people who were influenced by SFMF since its beginning. These stories from the first fifty years of SFMF not only chronicle the past but also give hope and direction to the future.

Reed, Lyan. 1985. *Preparing missionaries for intercultural communication: A bicultural approach.* Pasadena: William Carey Library.
     Missionaries, while being prepared in the Bible, often receive little training in understanding the world in which we live. Some experience great hardship out in the field as a result. The purpose of this book is to enable cross-cultural missionaries to be more adequately prepared for the task of intelligent communication.

Ridenour, Fritz. 1979. *So what's the difference?* Ventura: Regal.
     This short book explores the important contemporary concern (So what's the difference?) in a straightforward, noncritical comparison. It compares Roman Catholicism, Judaism, Islam, Hinduism, Buddhism, Unitarianism, Jehovah's Witnesses, Christian Science, and Mormonism with orthodox Christianity to show likenesses and differences. Christians must know the differences in order to defend their faith.

Robb, John. 1989. *Focus! The power of people group thinking.* London: MARC/WV Publishers.
     Briefly and beautifully, a scholar with dust on his boots explains the great value of taking note of subtle differences between people groups.

Rust, Brian, and Barry McLeish. 1984. *The support raising handbook.* Downers Grove, Ill.: InterVarsity.
     In this short book, Rust and McLeish answer questions on raising support with practical suggestions on developing an overall plan, listing possible supporters, keeping records, and determining methods of communication.

Roberts, W. Dayton, and John A. Siewart, eds. 1989. *Mission handbook.* Grand Rapids: Zondervan.
     This handbook is a report on the U.S.A. and Canadian Protestant Christian mission agencies and their activity outside of North America. The introductory essays offer a global overview, an analysis of parachurch structures, an update on tentmaking, a historical review of the associations of missions, and a statistical overview of the survey data. The directory chapters give basic information about each North American-based mission agency.

Seaton, Ronald S., and Edith B. Seaton. 1976. *Here's how: Health education by extension.* Pasadena: William Carey Library.
     Never in history has there been a more propitious time to unite in a single document the best thinking of the long-separated professions of physical and spiritual healing. This is a big, comprehensive book, valuable to all in responsible positions, especially in the world of mission service.

Shaw, Daniel. 1988. *Transculturation.* Pasadena: William Carey Library.
  This book lifts the track of translation of the Bible—or anything else—into the full complexity of the cultural factors that make it powerful. The author demonstrates that transculturation is a process of information transfer that takes the whole translation context into account and allows people to respond in a way that is natural and appropriate for them.

Shetler, Joanne, and Patricia Purvis. 1992. *And the Word came with power.* Portland: Multnomah.
  The dramatic story of how God set in motion events that brought Jo Shetler, of Wycliffe Bible Translators, together with the Balangao people, proud head-hunters who lived in the magnificent rice terraces of the Philippines. This book is about the power of God's Word that changed the lives of Balangaos forever and produced a strong Christian church that is growing and flourishing today.

Shibley, David. 1989. *A force in the earth.* Altamonte Springs, Fla.: Creation House.
  This is one of a very few books that deserves to be read by every red-blooded believer. Brimming over with excitement and optimism, jammed with up-to-the-minute information, this book cordially bridges the evangelical/charismatic boundary even though it is primarily addressed to the latter. It discusses the charismatic renewal and world evangelism.

Siewart, John, and John Kenyon, eds. 1993. *Mission handbook.* London: MARC/ World Vision.
  This new edition of the *Mission Handbook* reflects the changes of the new era— an era of changing communication and research methods, an era of a changing world order. John Siewart, co-editor, notes "agencies were more precise in their reporting. Missions are changing to meet the needs of the changing world. They are working to adjust to the new realities within a global perspective."

Steffen, Tom A. 1993. *Passing the baton.* La Habra: Center for Organizational and Ministry Development.
  This book shows how to plant and grow churches that will be responsible and productive. It shows personal role changes that missionaries must go through to empower national leadership. Steffen teaches the missionary how to develop reproducing churches even after the missionary leaves.

Swift, Catherine. 1989. *Gladys Aylward.* Minneapolis: Bethany House.
  The "Little Woman" whose great faith carried her to the people of China. Gladys Aylward's life is remembered around the world as one that defied all ex-pectations. Despite a poor education, and being told she was too old to learn the Chinese language, her desire to be a missionary refused to surrender its call. She went to China on her own, and what followed was one of the most remarkable missionary careers imaginable.

Torjesen, Edward P. 1983. *Fredrik Franson: Model for worldwide frontier evangelism.* Pasadena: William Carey Library.

Franson ranks with Hudson Taylor as one of few people who embraced mission as a movement to which he mightily contributed rather than see it in terms of a personal career. The author asks, then answers the question: "What biblical principle of vision, action, and organization did he [Franson] exemplify and propound that gave stability and permanence to his work and should have continual emphasis now?" A biographical work with much modern pertinence.

Tucker, Ruth. 1988. *Guardians of the great commission*. Grand Rapids: Zondervan.
  Focusing on women in missions, this book features accounts of daring pioneer missionaries, innovative concepts in mission strategy, and impassioned personal accounts of romance and intrigue.

Tullis, Wesley. 1988. *Mobilizer's notebook*. Pasadena: U.S. Center for World Missions.
  A beautiful two-hundred-page three-ring notebook bulging with a whole set of vital materials presented in many "Regional Mobilizers Workshops" across the country.

Van Engen, Charles. 1991. *God's missionary people*. Grand Rapids: Baker.
  A church growth and administration resource that instills a burden as well as facts and concepts. The author works through the realities of church life or denominational organization, but he seeks to present them in their kingdom perspective so Christians begin advancing a kingdom instead of maintaining a defensive fortress.

Vierow, Duane. 1977. *On the move . . . with the master*. Pasadena: William Carey Library.
  This devotional guide comes from the heart and experience of a diligent and fruitful missionary. It calls us to range widely over important scriptural themes, and relates them to the central task of the church. This is a daily devotional guide on world mission.

Wagner, C. Peter. 1985. *On the crest of the wave: Becoming a world Christian*. Ventura: Regal.
  Wagner states that "Some things in your life are optional and some are not. Becoming a Christian is an option, but once you have accepted Jesus Christ into your life, involvement in world mission is no longer optional." Much of this book is a review of *Stop the World I Want to Get On;* however, it does introduce you to some of the theological issues, creative strategies, spiritual resources, and practical steps needed for the final thrust of world evangelization.

————. 1981. *Stop the world I want to get on*. Pasadena: William Carey Library.
  "Every Christian is a witness," says C. Peter Wagner, "but not a missionary." This book reviews the Bible's teaching on spiritual gifts and helps you decide whether or not you are really a missionary—in case you happen to be one. It also talks about the need for muscle in the home church and takes a gook look at the contemporary issues on the front lines of mission development.

Wallstrom, Timothy C. 1980. *The creation of a student movement to evangelize the world*. Pasadena: William Carey International University Press.

This book was written to familiarize students with the origins of a vast and ambitious student missionary undertaking begun in the 1880s. Students interested in the world evangelism will find this book helpful, because much can be learned through the works of the predecessors (a history and analysis of the early stages of the student volunteer movements for foreign missionary).

Werning, Waldo. 1975. *The radical nature of Christianity*. Pasadena: William Carey Library.

This book deals with the asking for divine perspective, spiritual insight, and commitment by Christians to be instruments of the life-giving Spirit of God in a fast-moving age. It presents a practical strategy for continuing change and reform in individual lives and church structures.

Willis, Avery. 1977. *Indonesian revival*. Pasadena: William Carey Library.

A first-rate book that delves into the factors both functional and dysfunctional to the growth of the Javanese churches during the now-famous Indonesian Revival. The insights depicted in it must be studied by anyone seriously concerned about mission and church growth, and most of all, by every Indonesia-bound missionary.

Wilson, Christy. 1992. *More to be desired than gold*. South Hamilton, Mass.: Gordon-Conwell Books.

Billy Graham writes, "Countless successful preachers of the Gospel have used illustrations to help listeners better understand and come to experience God's presence in their everyday lives. These stories serve to illustrate that the real life experiences of Christians both at home and abroad are stranger than fiction. Not only do we value the marvelous things the Bible says, but I think you will enjoy reading here in this book about the amazing things that the Living God does."

————. 1979. *Today's tentmakers*. Wheaton: Tyndale.

An exciting, personalized account by an almost legendary figure, as well as a valuable tool for the prospective tentmaker or Christian in a secular job overseas. Information about foreign employment, support organizations, language training, cultural adjustment, and politics.

Winter, Ralph D., ed.-in-chief. 1993. *Mission frontiers*. Pasadena: Published monthly by U.S. Center for World Missions.

This is a bulletin of the U.S. Center for World Missions. It includes articles that are practical and useful for those who are interested in missions. There are sections of advertisement by different publishing companies and book reviews. It is a helpful resource.

Winter, Ralph D., and Steven C. Hawthorne, eds. 1992. *Perspectives on the world Christian movement: A reader*. Pasadena: William Carey Library.

God is raising up a new army of kingdom volunteers in our day and this book is a key tool. The editors have given to us an impressive (if not exhaustive) collection of readings that can help eager-hearted disciples to see world evangelization also in terms of passion, power, and participation. A 944-page book, but it has ninety-four different readings written by seventy-eight different authors that are short and helpful.

————. 1992. *Perspectives on the world Christian movement: A study guide.* Pasadena: William Carey Library.

A companion to *Perspectives on the World Christian Movement: A Reader,* this study guide takes you by the hand and walks you through the central issues dealt within the larger book. Includes questions, helpful comments, and additional readings.

*Is short-term mission really worth the time and money?* 1991. Published by Short Term Evangelical Missions Ministries (STEM).

This is a thirty-nine-page spiral-bound report findings of a study of changes in the perceptions and behavior of short-term mission participants as a result of, and subsequent to, their short-term mission experience with STEM. Substantial changes were found in prayer, financial giving, commitment to world mission, missions-related activities and education, and in feelings about returning to the mission field. These findings demonstrate an increase in participants' future contribution to the biblical mandate of world mission as a result.

*Missiology: An international review.* 1993. Scottdale, Penn.: American Society of Missiology.

This quarterly magazine is full of articles that are helpful to both short-term and long-term missionaries. The subjects of the articles vary each time. At the end of each journal there is a part called "Book Review." This section is very helpful for those who are searching for books related to certain topics.

*The 1992 great commission handbook.* 1992. Evanston, Ill.: Berry Publishing Services.

This annual magazine is filled with articles that are practical and helpful for the short-term missionary. It is also filled with a host of advertisements from educational and mission organizations advertising their trips and venues.

*Stepping out: A guide to short-term missions.* 1987. Monrovia: World Vision, Inc.

This magazine is published by World Vision to help broaden one's world view as related to missions. It has a number of articles but its primary focus seems to be advertisement for mission-related organizations.

*The short-term missions handbook.* 1992. Evanston, Ill.: Berry Publishing Services.

Published every three years, this magazine is a compilation of several years of articles from *The Great Commission Handbook.*

# International and North American Mission Organizations

## International Short-Term Mission Opportunities

| | | |
|---|---|---|
| Africa Evangelical Fellowship | P.O. Box 2896<br>Boone, NC 28607 | 704/264-6036 |
| Africa Inland Mission International | P.O. Box 178<br>Pearl River, NY 10965 | 914/735-4014 |
| Arab World Ministries | P.O. Box 96<br>Upper Darby, PA 19082 | 215/352-2003 |
| Azusa Pacific University<br>Institute of Outreach Ministries | 901 E. Alosta<br>Azusa, CA 91702 | 818/812-3027 |
| BALL World Missions | 8955 Old LeMay Ferry Road<br>Hillsboro, MO 63050 | 314/789-4368 |
| Baptist General Conference | 2002 S. Arlington Heights Rd.<br>Arlington, IL 60005 | 800/323-4215 |
| Calvary Commission | P.O. Box 100<br>Lindale, TX 75771 | 903/882-5501 |
| Campus Crusade for Christ<br>International<br>President's Office | 100 Sunport Lane<br>Orlando, FL 32809 | 800/444-5335 |
| Celebrant Singers | P.O. Box 1416<br>Visalia, CA 93279 | 800/321-2500 |
| Children's Haven International | 400 E. Minnesota Road<br>Pharr, TX 78577-9699 | 210/787-7378 |
| Christian Haitian Outreach | 6437 N.W. 22nd Court<br>Margate, FL 33063 | 305/972-3674 |
| Christian Outreach International | 12480 Wayzata Blvd.<br>Minnetonka, MN 55343 | 612/541-5343 |

| | | |
|---|---|---|
| Church of the Nazarene<br>Personnel Coordinator | 6401 The Paseo<br>Kansas City, MO 64131 | 816/333-7000 |
| CSI Ministires, Inc. | 804 W. McGalliard Road<br>Muncie, IN 47303-1764 | 317/286-0711 |
| DELTA Ministries International | P.O. Box 30029<br>Portland, OR 97230 | 800/5-DELTA-2 |
| Eastern European Outreach | P.O. Box 983<br>Sun City, CA 92586 | 714/244-4492 |
| Educational Services International | 1641 West Main Street, #401<br>Alhambra, CA 91801 | 818/284-7955 |
| English Learning Institute | P.O. Box 265<br>San Dimas, CA 91773 | 800/663-0372 |
| Evangelical Free Church of<br>America—Missions Dept. | 901 E. 78th Street<br>Minneapolis, MN 55420 | 800/745-2202 |
| Food for the Hungry<br>The Hunger Corps | 7729 East Greenway Road<br>Scottsdale, AZ 85260 | 800/2-HUNGER |
| Forward Edge International | 15121-A NE 72nd Ave.<br>Vancouver, WA 98686 | 206/574-3343 |
| Frontiers, Inc.<br>Summer Team Coordinator | 325 North Stapley Drive<br>Mesa, AZ 85203 | 800/GO-2-<br>THEM |
| Global Missions Fellowship | P.O. Box 742828<br>Dallas, TX 75374 | 214/783-7476 |
| Gospel Missionary Union | 1000 N. Oak Trafficway<br>Kansas City, MO 64155 | 816/734-8500 |
| Greater Europe Mission | P.O. Box 668<br>Wheaton, IL 60189 | 708/462-8050 |
| Harvest Evangelism, Inc. | P.O. Box 20310<br>San Jose, CA 95160 | 408/927-9052 |
| High School Evangelism Fellowship,<br>Inc. | P.O. Box 7<br>Bergenfield, NJ 07621 | 201/387-1750 |
| IMPACT Teams<br>University of the Nations | 75-5851 Kuakini Highway<br>Kailua-Kona, HI 96740 | 808/326-4464 |
| IMPACT Teams—Japan<br>University of the Nations | 75-5851 Kuakini Highway<br>Kailua-Kona, HI 96740 | 808/326-4464 |
| InterAct Ministries<br>(formerly Arctic Missions) | 31000 SE Kelso Road<br>Boring, OR 97009 | 800/258-3464 |
| International Family Missions | P.O. Box 309<br>Lafayette, CO 80026 | 303/665-7635 |
| International Messengers | 1600 Oak Hills Road SW<br>Bemidji, MN 56601 | 218/751-0388 |
| International Teams<br>Church Teams | P.O. Box 203<br>Prospect Heights, IL 0070 | 800/323-0428 |

| | | |
|---|---|---|
| International Teams<br>Moscow, Kazkhstan | P.O. Box 203<br>Prospect Heights, IL 0070 | 800/323-0428 |
| International Teams<br>Summer, 2-year, Career | P.O. Box 203<br>Prospect Heights, IL 60070 | 800/323-0428 |
| InterServe, USA | 239 Fairfield Ave<br>P.O. Box 418<br>Upper Darby, PA 19082-0418 | 215/352-0581 |
| Janz Team Ministries, Inc. | 2121 Henderson Hwy.<br>Winnipeg, MB R2G 1P8 | 204/334-0055 |
| Latin America Mission | P.O. Box 52-7900<br>Miami, FL 3152 | 800/275-8410 |
| Life Changers | P.O. Box 1103<br>Decatur, GA 30031 | 404/378-8746 |
| Life Investment | 14140 East Evans Ave.<br>Aurora, CO 80014 | 303/745-8191 |
| LIFE Ministries<br>Mobilization Dept. | P.O. Box 200<br>San Dimas, CA 91773 | 800/543-3678 |
| Living Water Teaching | P.O. Box 3040<br>Broken Arrow, OK 74013 | 800/541-2046 |
| Mercy Ships | P.O. Box 2020<br>Lindale, TX 75771 | 800/772-SHIP |
| Mexican Medical Ministries | P.O. Box 1847<br>Spring Valley, CA 91979 | 619/660-1106 |
| Missionary Dentists | P.O. Box 7002<br>Seattle, WA 8133 | 206/771-3241 |
| Missionary World Service and<br>Evangelism | P.O. Box 123<br>Wilmore, KY 40390 | 606/858-3171 |
| Missions Abroad Placement Service<br>(MAPS) Assemblies of God | 1445 Boonville Ave.<br>Springfield, MO 65802 | 417/862-2781 |
| The Navigators | P.O. Box 135<br>Warrenville, IL 60555 | 708/393-7800 |
| OMS International<br>Attn: NOW Corps and Crusade | P.O. Box A<br>Greenwood, IN 46142-6599 | 317/881-6751 |
| On The Go Ministries<br>Keith Cook Crusades | P.O. Box 963<br>Springfield, TN 37172 | 615/384-1881 |
| Operational Mobilization | P.O. Box 444<br>Tyrone, GA 30290 | 404/631-0432 |
| Overseas Missionary Fellowship—<br>SERVE ASIA | 10 West Dry Creek Circle<br>Littleton, CO 80120-4413 | 800/422-5330 |
| Pioneers | P.O. Box 527<br>Sterling, VA 0167 | 800/755-7284 |
| Royal Servants International | 5517 Warwick Place<br>Minneapolis, MN 55436-2467 | 612/925-3519 |

| | | |
|---|---|---|
| SEND International | Box 513<br>Farmington, MI 48332 | 313/477-4210<br>Ext. 109 |
| S.I.M. USA | Box 7900<br>Charlotte, NC 28241 | 800/521-6499 |
| South America Mission—InterSeed/<br>SEARCH | P.O. Box 6560<br>Lake Worth, FL 3466 | 407/965-1833 |
| South America Mission—Teachers | P.O. Box 6560<br>Lake Worth, FL 33466 | 407/965-1833 |
| Southern Baptist Convention,<br>Foreign Missions Board | P.O. Box 6767<br>Richmond, VA 23230 | 800/999-2889<br>Ext. 635 |
| SPRINT Ministries<br>c/o World Outreach Fellowship | P.O. Box 585603<br>Orlando, FL 32858-5603 | 407/425-5552 |
| STEM Ministries | P.O. Box 290066<br>Minneapolis, MN 55429 | 612/535-2944 |
| TEAM—The Evangelical Alliance<br>Mission | P.O. Box 969<br>Wheaton, IL 60189 | 708/653-5300 |
| Teen Mania Ministries | P.O. Box 700721<br>Tulsa, OK 74170-0721 | 918/496-1891 |
| Trans World Radio | P.O. Box 700<br>Cary, NC 27512 | 919/460-3700 |
| United Methodist Church<br>Volunteers in Mission Program | 475 Riverside Drive,<br>Room 1470<br>New York, NY 10115 | 800/654-5929 |
| Venture Teams International | #230, 720-28th St. N.E.<br>Calgary, AB | 800/543-9732 |
| WEC International | Box 1707<br>Ft. Washington, PA 19034 | 215/643-3414 |
| World Medical Mission | P.O. Box 3000<br>Boone, NC 28607 | 704/262-1980 |
| World Servants | 8233 Gator Lane #6<br>West Palm Beach, FL 33411 | 407/790-0800 |
| World Thrust, Inc. | P.O. Box 450105<br>Atlanta, GA 30345-0105 | 404/790-0800 |
| Wycliffe Associates, The Lay Ministry<br>of Wycliffe Bible Translators | Box 2000<br>Orange, CA 92669 | 714/639-9950 |
| Wycliffe Bible Translators | P.O. Box 2727<br>Huntington Beach, CA 92647 | 800/388-1928 |
| Youth for Christ—Project Serve | P.O. Box 228822<br>Denver, CO 80222 | 303/843-9000 |
| Youth With A Mission<br>North American Office | P.O. Box 55309<br>Seattle, WA 98155 | 206/363-9844 |
| Youth With A Mission—Amsterdam | Prins Hendrikkade 50,<br>1012 AC Amsterdam,<br>The Netherlands | 20/6269233 |

| | | |
|---|---|---|
| Youth With A Mission | P.O. Box 296<br>Sunland, CA 91041-0296 | 818/896-2755 |
| YUGO Ministries | P.O. Box 25<br>San Dimas, CA 91773 | 714/592-6621 |

# North American Short-Term Mission Opportunities

| | | |
|---|---|---|
| American Missionary Fellowship | 730 Leo Dr.<br>Santa Rosa, CA 95401 | 707/542-3761 |
| BCM International | 237 Fairfield Ave.<br>Upper Darby, PA 19082 | 215/353-7177 |
| Beyond Borders | P.O. Box 29612<br>Philadelphia, PA 19144 | 215/848-7102 |
| Center for Student Missions | P.O. Box 900<br>Dana Point, CA 92629 | 714/248-8200 |
| Child Evangelism Fellowship | P.O. Box 1449<br>Reseda, CA 91337 | 818/349-9883 |
| Christian Appalachian Project | 235 Lexington St.<br>Lancaster, KY 40444 | 800/755-5322 |
| Christian Haven Homes | Rt. 1, Box 17<br>Wheatfield, IN 46392 | 219/965-3125 |
| Christian Mission in the National Parks | 222 1/2 E. 49th St.<br>New York, NY 10017 | 212/758-3450 |
| Church Planting Int'l. | P.O. Box 1002<br>Cucamunga, CA 91730 | 714/945-1264 |
| City Teams Ministries | P.O. Box 143-HR44<br>San Jose, CA 95103 | 408/292-9406 |
| Construction Workers Christian Fellowship | 610 N. 1st Ave.<br>Kelso, WA 98626 | 206/423-5022 |
| Cornerstone Christian Academy | 1935-39 S. 58th St.<br>Philadelphia, PA 19143 | 215/341-1722 |
| The Fold, Inc. | P.O. Box 1188<br>Lyndonville, VT 05851 | 802/626-5620 |
| Gospel Missionary Union | 10000 N. Oak<br>Kansas City, MO 64155 | 800/GMU-1892 |
| Institute for Outreach Ministries | 901 E. Alosta<br>Azusa, CA 91702 | 818/812-3027 |
| Interact Ministries | 31000 SE Kelso Rd.<br>Boring, OR 97009 | 800/258-3464 |
| International Teams Inner City | P.O. Box 203<br>Prospect Heights, IL 60070 | 800/323-0428 |

| | | |
|---|---|---|
| International Union of Gospel Missions | 1045 Swift St. Kansas City, MO 64116 | 800/624-5156 |
| JAF Ministries | P.O. Box 3333 Agoura Hills, CA 91301 | 818/707-5664 |
| Jews for Jesus | 60 Haight St. San Francisco, CA 94102 | 415/864-2600 |
| Kingdomworks | P.O. Box 12589 Philadelphia, PA 19151 | 215-645-0800 |
| Koinonia Partners, Inc. | 1324 Highway 49 South Americus, GA 31709 | 912/924-0391 |
| Mountain T.O.P. Ministries, Inc. | 2704 12th Ave., South Nashville, TN 37201 | 615/298-1575 |
| NAIM Summer Ministries Institute | P.O. Box 151 Point Roberts, WA 98281 | 604/946-1227 |
| New Horizons Ministries | 1002 S. 350 East Marion, IN 46953 | 800/333-4009 |
| New York School of Urban Ministry | 31-65 46th St. Long Island City, NY 11103 | 718/204-6471 |
| Northern Canada Evangelical Mission | P.O. Box 3030 Prince Albert, SK S6V 7V4 | 306/764-3388 |
| Olive Branch Mission | 1043 W. Madison Chicago, IL 60607 | 312/243-3373 |
| Reaching Urban Neighborhoods | 501 Schoolhouse Rd. Telford, PA 18969 | 215/723-1590 |
| The Salvation Army | 615 Slaters Ln. Alexandria, VA 22313 | 703/684-5500 |
| Urban Promise | 3706 Westfield Ave. Camden, NJ 08110 | 609/964-5140 |
| Voice of Christ Ministries, Inc. | P.O. Box 474 Nenana, AK 99760 | 907/832-5426 |
| Voice of Calvary Ministries | 1655 St. Charles St. Jackson, MS 39209 | 601/944-0403 |
| World Impact | 2001 So. Vermont Ave. Los Angeles, CA 90007 | 213/735-1137 |
| World Relief | 201 Rt. 9W North Congers, NY 10920 | 800/647-6493 |